MANTRAS FOR THE MORNING

God's blessing + peace always,
Bp Bob Morn

MANTRAS
FOR THE
MORNING

An Introduction to Holistic Prayer

Robert F. Morneau

The Liturgical Press   Collegeville, Minnesota

Nihil obstat: Joseph C. Kremer, S.T.L., *Censor deputatus.*
Imprimatur: ✛George H. Speltz, D.D., Bishop of St. Cloud. February 9, 1981.
Copyright © 1981 by The Order of St. Benedict, Inc., Collegeville, Minnesota.

Library of Congress Cataloging in Publication Data

Morneau, Robert F., 1938–
    Mantras for the morning.

    1. Meditations. 2. Prayers. I. Title. II. Title: Holistic prayer.
BX2182.2.M668   242   81-1085
ISBN 0-8146-1210-5 (pbk.)   AACR2

CONTENTS

6 Contents

ACKNOWLEDGMENTS

The author owes particular gratitude to the following, who contributed their time and talent to make this book possible:

REV. ROBERT LALIBERTE AND REV. JOHN BLAHA, for their photography; SISTER MIRIAM CECILE ROSS, S.S.N.D., for the music; SISTER JANICE STINGLE, O.S.F., for her many hours of typing; SISTER MARIE ISABEL MC ELRONE, O.S.F., and SISTER MARY DE SALES HOFFMANN, O.S.F., for their friendly, critical eyes.

Grateful acknowledgment is made to the following for permission to include copyrighted material:

THE BODLEY HEAD, LTD.: *Diary of a Country Priest,* by Georges Bernanos (British and Commonwealth rights, excluding Canada).

CROWN PUBLISHERS, INC.: *The Crystal Arrow,* by Félix Martí-Ibáñez.

DAVID MC KAY CO., INC.: *The Simone Weil Reader,* edited by George A. Panichas. Copyright © 1977.

DODD, MEAD & COMPANY: *The Hound of Heaven,* by Francis Thompson.

DOUBLEDAY & COMPANY, INC.: *The Human Adventure,* by William McNamara, O.C.D. Copyright © 1974 by William McNamara. *The Confessions of St. Augustine,* translated by John K. Ryan. Copyright © 1960 by Doubleday & Company, Inc. *The Cloud of Unknowing and the Book of Privy Counseling,* edited by William Johnston. Copyright © 1973 by William Johnston. *The Genesee Diary,* by Henri Nouwen. Copyright © 1976 by Henri J. M. Nouwen. *Anne Frank: The Diary of a Young Girl.* Copyright © 1952 by Otto H. Frank.

HARCOURT BRACE JOVANOVICH, INC.: *The Little Prince,* by Antoine de Saint-Exupéry.

HOLT, RINEHART & WINSTON, INC.: *Mister God, This Is Anna,* by Fynn. Copyright © 1974 by Fynn.

IGS PUBLICATIONS: *The Collected Works of St. John of the Cross,* translated by Kieran Kavanaugh and Otilio Rodriguez. Copyright © 1964, 1979 by the Washington Province of Discalced Carmelites, Inc.

LITTLE, BROWN AND COMPANY and HARVARD UNIVERSITY PRESS: *The Poems of Emily Dickinson.* Reprinted by permission of the publishers and the Trustees of Amherst College from *The Poems of Emily Dickinson,* edited by Thomas H. Johnson, Cambridge, Mass.: The Belknap Press of Harvard University Press. Copyright © 1951, 1955, 1979 by the President and Fellows of Harvard College.

7

MACMILLAN PUBLISHING CO., INC.: *Diary of a Country Priest,* by Georges Bernanos (American and Canadian rights). Copyright © 1937 and renewed 1965 by Macmillan Publishing Co., Inc. *The Word: Readings in Theology,* by Karl Rahner et al. Copyright © 1964 by Macmillan Publishing Co., Inc.

ORBIS BOOKS: *Christology at the Crossroads,* by Jon Sobrino, S.J. Copyright © 1978.

OXFORD UNIVERSITY PRESS: *Beowulf,* in *An Anthology of Old English Poetry,* translated by Charles W. Kennedy. Copyright © 1960.

PAULIST PRESS: *Julian of Norwich: Showings* (Classics of Western Spirituality), translated by Edmond Colledge, O.S.A., and James Walsh, S.J. Copyright © 1978 by The Missionary Society of St. Paul the Apostle in the State of New York.

RANDOM HOUSE, INC.: *The Divine Comedy,* translated by Lawrence Grant White. *The Living God,* by Romano Guardini. *Witness,* by Whittaker Chambers.

THE SEABURY PRESS, INC.: *Collection: Papers by Bernard Lonergan.* Copyright © 1967 by the author.

SHEED & WARD, LTD., London: *The Complete Works of St. Teresa of Jesus,* translated by E. Allison Peers.

WAKE-BROOK HOUSE: *Some Did Return,* by Ruth Mary Fox.

A. P. WATT, LTD.: *St. Francis of Assisi,* by G. K. Chesterton.

Scripture texts used in this book are taken from:

The Jerusalem Bible, used by permission of Doubleday & Company, Inc. Copyright © 1966 by Darton, Longman & Todd, Ltd., London, and Doubleday & Company, Inc.

The New American Bible, copyright © 1970 by the Confraternity of Christian Doctrine, Washington, D.C., used by permission of said copyright owner. No part of the *New American Bible* may be reproduced in any form without permission in writing from the Confraternity of Christian Doctrine, Washington, D.C.

The Psalms, copyright © The Grail (England) 1963 and published by Collins, 1963. Used by permission.

INTRODUCTION

IN RECENT YEARS many voices in education, business, and medicine have been promoting a holistic approach to the human person. Teachers, they urge, must not only impart information to their students but also help them to integrate their emotions and to act maturely. Thus the cognitive, affective, and behavioral dimensions receive due attention in the education of the whole person. Employers, too, realize that their employees will produce more if they are physically fit and psychologically stable. Some businesses, therefore, provide recreational facilities and counseling services for their workers. Those in the medical field realize that care for the total person will contribute to the restoration or maintenance of good health. They see the patient as much more than a sick body; besides proper physical care, the psychological and spiritual needs of the patient have become concerns in the healing process.

Spiritual growth, too, is a holistic process. It involves all our relationships—with God, with others, with ourselves, and even with nature. Spiritual experiences involve the head, the heart, and the hands. Central to these experiences is prayer, the dialogic process with God. Authentic prayer is not just a head trip or an emotional experience or a moral exercise—it is all these and more. The *whole* person comes to prayer. The stimulus to prayer must be sufficient to allow for the full human participation of the individual or the community.

Prayer is essentially an encounter with God. Ideally, this encounter should elicit a total response from the one praying. Realistically, however, the prayer experience that takes as its stimulus a personal experience, a selection from Scripture, or a meditative reading does not address itself to the whole person but rather to a single dimension of our being: an idea to touch the mind, a song to move the heart, a picture to create a mood, a summary statement to incite an action. In this book we want to provide stimuli for prayer experiences that involve the whole person. When our encounter with God embraces the cognitive, affective, and behavioral aspects of our lives, we will enjoy an integrated spirituality.

9

Methodology

Twenty-five themes are presented for prayerful reflection. Such themes as simplicity, indwelling, intimacy, and presence are universal. Each theme is encapsulated in a mantra (a phrase or statement of seven syllables to be rhythmically repeated in order to center oneself in prayer or on a single point). The mantra serves as a technique for holding attention, for achieving simplicity in prayer, and for providing unity. As we repeat the mantra reverently and thoughtfully, it becomes a part of our internal timing. Synchronized with our breathing, the mantra resonates at a depth that can touch the very essence of our lives. Furthermore, the mantra helps us to slow down, to journey deep within, to feel the pulse of our inner life, to live from a deeper source. "Dearest freshness deep down things," taken from Hopkins's poem "God's Grandeur," is such a mantra. To ponder this insight, to feel its movement, to begin to perceive and respond to its truth fosters fullness of life.

The source of these mantras is either Scripture (primarily psalms) or faith poetry. The mantra is stated and then presented in the more meaningful context of the full psalm or poem. This prayer stimulus is then supported by parallel references from the Scriptures that further develop the basic theme and enlarge upon the mantra.

A threefold expansion is then given. A photograph allows us to see experientially how the theme-mantra is found in nature or in human interactions. If indeed a picture is worth many words, then we benefit greatly in using our sight to capture the tone and beauty that escape words. Another advantage is that pictures and images tend to draw us more deeply into life because of their concreteness and familiarity.

A second dimension of the theme-mantra is presented in an appeal to our hearing. Within the verbal silence of the mantra resides a song (more accurately, many songs, depending upon the listeners and the season of one's heart). A single melody, gently extracted from the mantra, allows the power of music to stir the heart and inspire the soul. Deep affectivity resides in music; indeed, all prayer is essentially a song, and the strongest prayer is affective in nature.

The third dimension of the theme-mantra is seen in the written word. The mantra, repeated many times in double lines, journeys into a variety of areas in an attempt to touch concrete human experiences. The intent here is to allow the reader to discover deeper meaning more through poetic intuition than through philosophical reasoning. Images, personalities, and localities are the references offered in order to foster a prayer based more on the particular than on the universal, more on the concrete than on the abstract.

The theme-mantra experienced in its photographic, musical, and verbal dimensions is followed by a short prayer for the grace to live out the theme under consideration. Here the behavioral aspect of spirituality is stressed, and a challenge is presented to our lifestyles. Thus we see the two sides of prayer: the inward journey of being with the Father and the outward thrust of being sent to live the word pondered. Through the visual, auditory, and verbal avenues, the totality of our personality is drawn into the spiritual experience.

Each theme-mantra is then concluded with a series of quotations from various authors: poets, mystics, philosophers, theologians, novelists. In their writings they have articulated some insight that further enriches the theme chosen for prayer. These quotations confirm the significance of the theme and highlight some of its aspects. These quotations in and of themselves might well serve as stimuli for future prayer experiences.

Newness

MANTRA: **Dearest freshness deep down things**

SOURCE: Gerard Manley Hopkins, "God's Grandeur"

The world is charged with the grandeur of God.
 It will flame out, like shining from shook foil;
 It gathers to a greatness, like the ooze of oil
Crushed. Why do men then now not reck his rod?
Generations have trod, have trod, have trod;
 And all is seared with trade; bleared, smeared with toil;
 And wears man's smudge and shares man's smell: the soil
Is bare now, nor can foot feel, being shod.

And for all this, nature is never spent;
 There lives the dearest freshness deep down things;
And though the last lights off the black West went
 Oh, morning, at the brown brink eastward, springs—
Because the Holy Ghost over the bent
 World broods with warm breast and with ah! bright wings.[1]

PARALLEL REFERENCES

Finally, brothers, fill your minds with everything that is true, everything that is noble, everything that is good and pure, everything that we love and honor, and everything that can be thought virtuous or worthy of praise. *(Philippians 4:8)*

You give breath, fresh life begins,
you keep renewing the world. *(Psalm 104:30)*

No doubt of it, but God reveals wonders,
and does great deeds that we cannot understand. *(Job 37:5)*

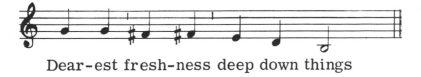

Dear-est fresh-ness deep down things

INWARD JOURNEY

The quiet moment of dawn,
The wrinkled grandpa hand,
The tender, gentle kiss,
    DEAREST FRESHNESS DEEP DOWN THINGS,
    DEAREST FRESHNESS DEEP DOWN THINGS.

The scar of years gone by,
The fading memory,
The blurring of vision,
    DEAREST FRESHNESS DEEP DOWN THINGS,
    DEAREST FRESHNESS DEEP DOWN THINGS.

A March breeze,
Oil crossed on forehead,
The dog's velvet ear,
    DEAREST FRESHNESS DEEP DOWN THINGS,
    DEAREST FRESHNESS DEEP DOWN THINGS.

The rediscovered love letter,
The inadequate phone call,
A July ice cube,
    DEAREST FRESHNESS DEEP DOWN THINGS,
    DEAREST FRESHNESS DEEP DOWN THINGS.

The candle flame,
A hurrying wave,
Grosbeaks stealing cherries,
    DEAREST FRESHNESS DEEP DOWN THINGS,
    DEAREST FRESHNESS DEEP DOWN THINGS.

A simple meal,
A tear and a fear,
A friend's care,
    DEAREST FRESHNESS DEEP DOWN THINGS,
    DEAREST FRESHNESS DEEP DOWN THINGS.

Dear-est fresh-ness deep down things

PRAYER

Father, hidden just beyond our gaze is mystery, the mystery of your presence and love. Send your Spirit into our hearts that we may see what is invisible to the eye and touch what our hands cannot feel. Through Jesus our Lord we come to know the deep down things of life and to delight in their dearest freshness. Father, we praise you!

QUOTATIONS

Flower in the crannied wall,
I pluck you out of the crannies,
I hold you here, root and all, in my hand,
Little flower — but if I could understand
What you are, root and all, and all in all,
I should know what God and man is. *(Alfred Lord Tennyson)*[2]

Presently, God said,
"And what did you do?"
The little blade answered, "Oh, my Lord,
Memory is bitter to me,
For, if I did good deeds,
I know not of them."
Then God, in all His splendor,
Arose from His throne.
"O best little blade of grass!" He said. *(Stephen Crane)*[3]

That we are dependent in every detail, at every instant, as a Christian would say, upon God, as even an agnostic would say, upon existence and the nature of things, is not an illusion of imagination; on the contrary, it is the fundamental fact which we cover up, as with curtains, with the illusion of ordinary life. *(G. K. Chesterton)*[4]

The Promise

MANTRA: **I have promised, says the Lord**

SOURCE: Ezekiel 37:12-14

Thus says the Lord God: O my people, I will open your graves and have you rise from them, and bring you back to the land of Israel. Then you shall know that I am the Lord, when I open your graves and have you rise from them, O my people! I will put my spirit in you that you may live, and I will settle you upon your land; thus you shall know that I am the Lord. I have promised, and I will do it, says the Lord.

PARALLEL REFERENCES

Yahweh said to Abram, "Leave your country, your family and your father's house, for the land I will show you. I will make you a great nation; I will bless you and make your name so famous that it will be used as a blessing.

> "I will bless those who bless you:
> I will curse those who slight you.
> All the tribes of the earth
> shall bless themselves by you." *(Genesis 12:1-3)*

Now you too, in him,
have heard the message of the truth and the good news of your
    salvation,
and have believed it;
and you too have been stamped with the seal of the Holy Spirit
    of the Promise,
the pledge of our inheritance
which brings freedom for those whom God has taken for his own,
to make his glory praised. *(Ephesians 1:13-14)*

Everyone moved by the Spirit is a son of God. The spirit you received is not the spirit of slaves bringing fear into your lives again; it is the spirit of sons, and it makes us cry out, "Abba, Father!" The Spirit himself and our spirit bear united witness that we are children of God. And if we are children we are heirs as well: heirs of God and coheirs with Christ, sharing his sufferings so as to share his glory. *(Romans 8:14-17)*

I have prom - ised, says the Lord

INWARD JOURNEY

Death shall lose its sting,
Tears shall be wiped away,
Hope shall fill the land,
    I HAVE PROMISED . . . SAYS THE LORD,
    I HAVE PROMISED . . . SAYS THE LORD.

      No rose garden here,
      No crossless journey,
      Only crosses of glory,
        I HAVE PROMISED . . . SAYS THE LORD,
        I HAVE PROMISED . . . SAYS THE LORD.

          I will be with you always,
          I will be in you forever,
          I will be for you eternally,
            I HAVE PROMISED . . . SAYS THE LORD,
            I HAVE PROMISED . . . SAYS THE LORD.

Lazarus, come forth,
Martha, do not weep,
Mary, regain your hope,
    I HAVE PROMISED . . . SAYS THE LORD,
    I HAVE PROMISED . . . SAYS THE LORD.

      Paul, arise from the dust,
      Stephen, see the open heavens,
      Mary, I called you by name,
        I HAVE PROMISED . . . SAYS THE LORD,
        I HAVE PROMISED . . . SAYS THE LORD.

          You, my people, O my people,
          Branded on my hands,
          Share my heart and life,
            I HAVE PROMISED . . . SAYS THE LORD,
            I HAVE PROMISED . . . SAYS THE LORD.

PRAYER

Father, you call us your people
   and promise us life and the gift of your Spirit.
Jesus, you fulfill the promise of your Father
   in Bethany, Naim, and Calvary.
Spirit of the Father and Son, help us to live
   on the promise of eternal life.
   Help us to be open to your movements
   deep within our being.
Yes! Amen! Alleluia!

QUOTATIONS

"The Cheyennes do not break their word," One-Eye replied.
"If they should do so, I would not care to live longer."
(Dee Brown)[5]

To any kind of promise men now flock. *(Dante)*[6]

Death, be not proud, though some have called thee
Mighty and dreadful, for thou art not so;
For those whom thou think'st thou dost overthrow
Die not, poor Death; nor yet canst thou kill me.
From rest and sleep, which but thy picture be,
Much pleasure; then from thee much more must flow;
And soonest our best men with thee do go—
Rest of their bones and souls' delivery!
Thou 'rt slave to fate, chance, kings, and desperate men,
And dost with poison, war, and sickness dwell;
And poppy or charms can make us sleep as well
And better than thy stroke. Why swell'st thou then?
One short sleep past, we wake eternally,
And death shall be no more: Death, thou shalt die! *(John Donne)*[7]

Listening

MANTRA: **If you hearken to my voice**

SOURCE: Exodus 19:3-7

Moses went up the mountain to God. Then the Lord called to him and said, "Thus shall you say to the house of Jacob; tell the Israelites: You have seen for yourselves how I treated the Egyptians and how I bore you up on eagle wings and brought you here to myself. Therefore, if you hearken to my voice and keep my covenant, you shall be my special possession, dearer to me than all other people, though all the earth is mine. You shall be to me a kingdom of priests, a holy nation. That is what you must tell the Israelites."

PARALLEL REFERENCES

Come, let us bow down in worship;
   let us kneel before the Lord who made us.
For he is our God,
   and we are the people he shepherds, the flock he guides.

Oh, that today you would hear his voice:
   "Harden not your hearts as at Meribah,
   as in the day of Massah in the desert,
Where your fathers tempted me;
   they tested me though they had seen my works." *(Psalm 95:6-9)*

. . . they have forsaken my Law which I put before them and have not listened to my voice or followed it, but have followed the dictates of their own stubborn hearts, followed the Baals as their ancestors taught them. *(Jeremiah 9:12-14)*

Oh, come to the water all you who are thirsty;
though you have no money, come!
Buy corn without money, and eat,
and, at no cost, wine and milk.

Why spend money on what is not bread,
your wages on what fails to satisfy?
Listen, listen to me, and you will have good things to eat
and rich food to enjoy.
Pay attention, come to me;
listen, and your soul will live. *(Isaiah 55:1-3)*

If you heark-en to my voice

INWARD JOURNEY

The desert is cold,
There is no food,
Water cannot be found.
IF YOU HEARKEN TO MY VOICE,
IF YOU HEARKEN TO MY VOICE.

Another land was hard,
Yet food and water were there.
Our bodies lived
Though our souls were dead.
IF YOU HEARKEN TO MY VOICE,
IF YOU HEARKEN TO MY VOICE.

Why did we leave?
Why forced from our slavery?
There is no freedom without comfort.
Take us back "home."
IF YOU HEARKEN TO MY VOICE,
IF YOU HEARKEN TO MY VOICE.

Where is our God?
Is there a where to God?
God who?
Is the Lord in our midst or not?
IF YOU HEARKEN TO MY VOICE,
IF YOU HEARKEN TO MY VOICE.

IF YOU HEARKEN TO MY VOICE,
IF YOU HEARKEN TO MY VOICE.
Expose your heart to the desert air,
Empty it freely,
Empty it in hope.

IF YOU HEARKEN TO MY VOICE,
IF YOU HEARKEN TO MY VOICE.
   Cry out for living water,
   Catch the spirit in silence,
   Come in your poverty for richness.

IF YOU HEARKEN TO MY VOICE,
IF YOU HEARKEN TO MY VOICE.
   Sing a song of poverty,
   Sing of silence and hope,
   Silently sing.

IF YOU HEARKEN TO MY VOICE,
IF YOU HEARKEN TO MY VOICE.
   His voice is heard!
   His heart is given!
   His hand reaches out!

If you heark-en to my voice

PRAYER

   Faithful Yahweh, you lead us into the desert
     to speak to our restless hearts.
   Compel us to go there like your Son,
     driven and led by the Spirit.
   In our emptiness fill our hearts;
     in our despair, give us hope;
     in our restlessness, give us peace.
   Grant this in Jesus' name. Amen.

QUOTATIONS

It was one of the ferryman's greatest virtues that, like few people, he knew how to listen. *(Hermann Hesse)*[8]

Offer him your heart in a soft and tractable state, and preserve the form in which the Creator has fashioned you, having moisture in yourself lest, by becoming hardened, you lose the impressions of his fingers. *(Ladislaus Boros)*[9]

And he went back to meet the fox.

"Goodbye," he said.

"Goodbye," said the fox. "And now here is my secret, a very simple secret: It is only with the heart that one can see rightly; what is essential is invisible to the eye."

"What is essential is invisible to the eye," the little prince repeated so that he would be sure to remember. *(Antoine de Saint-Exupéry)*[10]

Contentment

MANTRA: **There is nothing I shall want**

SOURCE: Psalm 23

The Lord is my shepherd;
there is nothing I shall want.
Fresh and green are the pastures
where he gives me repose,
Near restful waters he leads me,
To revive my drooping spirit.

He guides me along the right path;
he is true to his name.
If I should walk in the valley of darkness
no evil would I fear.
You are there with your crook and your staff;
with these you give me comfort.

You have prepared a banquet for me
in the sight of my foes.
My head you have anointed with oil;
my cup is overflowing.

Surely goodness and kindness shall follow me
all the days of my life.
In the Lord's own house shall I dwell
for ever and ever.

PARALLEL REFERENCES

I am the good shepherd:
the good shepherd is one who lays down his life for his sheep.
(John 10:11)

For him I have accepted the loss of everything,
and I look on everything as so much rubbish
if only I can have Christ and be given a place in him.
(Philippians 3:8)

Preserve me, God, I take refuge in you.
I say to the Lord: "You are my God.
My happiness lies in you alone." *(Psalm 16:1-2)*

There is noth-ing I shall want

INWARD JOURNEY

Samuel came to me
With oil and horn and wonder,
The Lord's spirit rushed me over.
THERE IS NOTHING I SHALL WANT,
THERE IS NOTHING I SHALL WANT.

Jesus came to me
With light and love and life,
The Lord's spirit conquered darkness.
THERE IS NOTHING I SHALL WANT,
THERE IS NOTHING I SHALL WANT.

Sabbath Christ came to me
With mud and joy and freedom,
The Lord's spirit blinded my soul.
THERE IS NOTHING I SHALL WANT,
THERE IS NOTHING I SHALL WANT.

David's heart was full,
His sheep tenderly loved,
His spirit, like ours, chosen by him.
THERE IS NOTHING I SHALL WANT,
THERE IS NOTHING I SHALL WANT.

Paul's vision was clear,
His children called to see,
His spirit, like ours, awakened by him.
THERE IS NOTHING I SHALL WANT,
THERE IS NOTHING I SHALL WANT.

The blind man was healed,
His parents found and questioned,
His spirit, like ours, steeped in grace.
THERE IS NOTHING I SHALL WANT,
THERE IS NOTHING I SHALL WANT.

PRAYER OF THE BLIND MAN

Lord Jesus, you shepherd us, your people. You restore our sight.
Inflame our hearts. Call us to worship and service. Continue to
heal our blindness. Never let our hearts grow cold. Empower us to

reach out to you and our brothers and sisters. May you be praised by all, especially those healed of blindness. Amen.

QUOTATIONS

. . . when I am but happy, I ask for no more. *(Søren Kierkegaard)*[11]

The Renaissance substituted an anthropocentric humanism for the theocentric humanism of the middle ages; and though this shifting of the centre of life was expected to issue in a new age of happiness and perfection for man, in point of fact it excluded two essential elements of the good life, without which happiness is in fact impossible: creatureliness and creativity. *(Gerald Vann)*[12]

These, precisely, are the greedy. Their appetite and joy is already so extended and dispersed among creatures — and with such anxiety — that they cannot be satisfied. The more their appetite and thirst increases, the further they regress from God, the fount which alone can satisfy them. *(St. John of the Cross)*[13]

Remember, too, that the more his heart is trained to be sensitive to divine influences, the happier man is; the further he pushes his preparation, the higher he ascends in the scale of happiness.
(Meister Eckhart)[14]

There is noth - ing I shall want

Pleasing God

MANTRA: **What is pleasing in your eyes**

SOURCE: Wisdom 9:1-10

God of our ancestors, Lord of mercy,
who by your word have made all things,
and in your wisdom have fitted man
to rule the creatures that have come from you,
to govern the world in holiness and justice
and in honesty of soul to wield authority,
grant me Wisdom, consort of your throne,
and do not reject me from the number of your children.

For I am your servant, son of your serving maid,
a feeble man, with little time to live,
with small understanding of justice and the laws.
Indeed, were anyone perfect among the sons of men,
if he lacked the Wisdom that comes from you, he would still
   count for nothing.
You yourself have chosen me to be king over your people,
to be judge of your sons and daughters.
You have bidden me build a temple on your holy mountain,
an altar in the city where you have pitched your tent,
a copy of that sacred tabernacle which you prepared from the
   beginning.
With you is Wisdom, she who knows your works,
she who was present when you made the world;
she understands what is pleasing in your eyes
and what agrees with your commandments.
Dispatch her from the holy heavens,
send her forth from your throne of glory
to help me and to toil with me
and teach me what is pleasing to you,
since she knows and understands everything.

29

PARALLEL REFERENCES

"My Father," he said, "if this cup cannot pass by without my drinking it, your will be done." *(Matthew 26:42)*

Such is the richness of the grace
which he has showered on us
in all wisdom and insight.
He has let us know the mystery of his purpose,
the hidden plan he so kindly made in Christ from the beginning.
(Ephesians 1:8-9)

What is pleas - ing in your eyes

INWARD JOURNEY

A deed just and right,
A love tender and bright,
A faith simple and light.
> WHAT IS PLEASING IN YOUR EYES,
> WHAT IS PLEASING IN YOUR EYES.

Slaves' bonds broken,
Words softly spoken,
Prayer seeds woken,
> WHAT IS PLEASING IN YOUR EYES,
> WHAT IS PLEASING IN YOUR EYES.

Water graciously given,
Tears compassionately driven,
Sins mercifully shriven,
> WHAT IS PLEASING IN YOUR EYES,
> WHAT IS PLEASING IN YOUR EYES.

Shelter, heart desires,
Touches, love inspires,
Whispers, dawn admires.
> WHAT IS PLEASING IN YOUR EYES,
> WHAT IS PLEASING IN YOUR EYES.

Ghettos eternally banished,
Pilgrims no longer famished,
Incense nevermore vanished.
> WHAT IS PLEASING IN YOUR EYES,
> WHAT IS PLEASING IN YOUR EYES.

A deed just and right,
A love tender and bright,
A faith simple and light.
> WHAT IS PLEASING IN YOUR EYES,
> WHAT IS PLEASING IN YOUR EYES.

PRAYER

Father, grant us wisdom that we may come to know
  what is truly pleasing in your eyes.
Jesus, Wisdom of the Father, empower us to follow
  in your way.
Spirit of love and justice, instill within all of us
  the desire to serve generously and totally.

What is pleas - ing in your eyes

QUOTATIONS

Then He said to me: "Ah, daughter, how few are they who love Me
in truth! If people loved Me, I should not hide my secrets from
them. Knowest thou what it is to love Me in truth? It is to realize
that everything which is not pleasing to Me is a lie. Thou dost not
yet realize this, but thou shalt come to see it clearly in the profit it
will bring to thy soul." *(St. Teresa of Avila)*[15]

Those who really love God love all good, seek all good, help
forward all good, praise all good, and invariably join forces with
good men and help and defend them. They love only truth and
things worthy of love. Do you think it possible that anyone who
really and truly loves God can love vanities, riches, worldly
pleasures or honors? Can he engage in strife or feel envy? No, for
his only desire is to please the Beloved. *(St. Teresa of Avila)*[16]

It was a direct look of the utmost compassion. It withheld judgment. It recognized human nature. Her eyes looked dark blue instead of blue-gray. She had no need to speak in words the feeling
which then showed in her eyes. *(Paul Horgan)*[17]

The Prophet

MANTRA: **For he has anointed me**

SOURCE: Luke 4:16-22

He came to Nazara, where he had been brought up, and went into the synagogue on the sabbath day as he usually did. He stood up to read, and they handed him the scroll of the prophet Isaiah. Unrolling the scroll he found the place where it is written:
> The spirit of the Lord has been given to me,
> for he has anointed me.
> He has sent me to bring the good news to the poor,
> to proclaim liberty to captives
> and to the blind new sight,
> to set the downtrodden free,
> to proclaim the Lord's year of favor.

He then rolled up the scroll, gave it back to the assistant and sat down. And all eyes in the synagogue were fixed on him. Then he began to speak to them, "This text is being fulfilled today even as you listen." And he won the approval of all, and they were astonished by the gracious words that came from his lips.

PARALLEL REFERENCES

The spirit of the Lord Yahweh has been given to me,
for Yahweh has anointed me.
He has sent me to bring good news to the poor,
to bind up hearts that are broken;

to proclaim liberty to captives,
freedom to those in prison;
to proclaim a year of favor from Yahweh,
a day of vengeance for our God. *(Isaiah 61:1-2)*

Elijah the Tishbite, of Tishbe in Gilead, said to Ahab, "As Yahweh lives, the God of Israel whom I serve, there shall be neither dew nor rain these years except at my order." The word of Yahweh came to him, "Go away from here, go eastward, and hide yourself in the wadi Cherith which lies east of Jordan." *(1 Kings 17:1-3)*

The brotherhood of prophets saw him in the distance, and said, "The spirit of Elijah has come to rest on Elisha"; they went to meet him and bowed to the ground before him. *(2 Kings 2:15)*

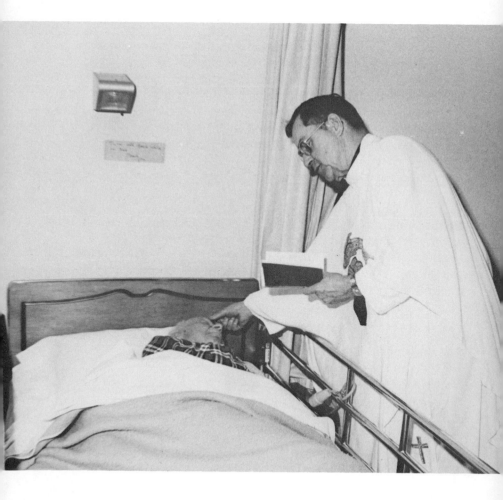

For he has a - noint - ed me

INWARD JOURNEY

My name is Isaiah.
I see a broken and empty land,
I come to free and heal,
    FOR HE HAS ANOINTED ME,
    FOR HE HAS ANOINTED ME.

My name is Elijah.
I see a land of desolation and hunger,
I come to bring water and life,
    FOR HE HAS ANOINTED ME,
    FOR HE HAS ANOINTED ME.

My name is Elisha.
I see the pain of illness and decay,
I come to heal and restore,
    FOR HE HAS ANOINTED ME,
    FOR HE HAS ANOINTED ME.

My name is Jesus.
I see people in darkness,
I come to bring love and hope,
    FOR HE HAS ANOINTED ME,
    FOR HE HAS ANOINTED ME.

My name is . . .
I see . . .
I come . . .
    FOR HE HAS ANOINTED ME,
    FOR HE HAS ANOINTED ME.

For he has a - noint - ed me

PRAYER

God our Father, in your goodness and concern for the world, you anoint and consecrate messengers who are sent to share your life and love. Jesus is *the* prophet; we are called to put on his mind and heart and to share in his anointing. May your Spirit be upon us. Grant this through your Son, our Lord Jesus.

QUOTATIONS

If we are to ascertain the success or failure of Christianity, we must know exactly what the mission of Christ is. His mission is twofold: to show forth the Father and to unite us with the Godhead. In this way he satisfies man's twofold basic human need for intuition and for vital union. A man loves to see, admire, and contemplate good, beautiful things; he also loves to become in some way equated or identified with them. Thus you have always in the face of the true, the good, and the beautiful (wine, food, music, a woman, a man) the need for intuition and union. The mission of Christianity, therefore, is to enable man to see God and to be with God.

(William McNamara)[18]

When a man lives with God, his voice shall be as sweet as the murmur of the brook and the rustle of the corn.

(Ralph Waldo Emerson)[19]

We are reminded of the conflict that is the prophet's constant lot. He stands squarely in the turmoil of a daily life moved by necessity, pleasure and earthly values. Men desire to eat and drink; to live and possess; to work, create, reap honor and power. In a world of such desires, comprehensible to all, the prophet is necessarily a foreign body. *(Romano Guardini)*[20]

The Smile

MANTRA: **Did he smile his work to see?**

SOURCE: William Blake, "The Tiger"

Tiger, Tiger, burning bright
In the forest of the night,
What immortal hand or eye
Could frame thy fearful symmetry?

In what distant deeps or skies
Burned the fire of thine eyes?
On what wings dared he aspire?
What the hand dare seize the fire?

And what shoulder, and what art,
Could twist the sinews of thy heart?
When thy heart began to beat,
What dread hand forged thy dread feet?

What the hammer? What the chain?
Knit thy strength and forged thy brain?
What the anvil? What dread grasp
Dared its deadly terrors clasp?

When the stars threw down their spears,
And watered heaven with their tears,
Did he smile his work to see?
Did he who made the lamb make thee?

Tiger, Tiger, burning bright
In the forest of the night,
What immortal hand or eye
Could frame thy fearful symmetry?[21]

PARALLEL REFERENCES

Jesus looked steadily at him [the rich young man] and loved him, and he said, "There is one thing you lack. Go and sell everything you own and give the money to the poor, and you will have treasure in heaven; then come, follow me." *(Mark 10:21)*

And so it was. God saw all he had made, and indeed it was very good. Evening came and morning came: the sixth day. *(Genesis 1:31)*

As soon as Jesus was baptized he came up from the water, and suddenly the heavens opened and he saw the Spirit of God descending like a dove and coming down on him. And a voice spoke from heaven, "This is my Son, the Beloved; my favor rests on him."
(Matthew 3:16-17)

Did he smile his work to see?

INWARD JOURNEY

A tiger and a lamb,
A flower and a weed,
A tear and a laugh,
 DID HE SMILE HIS WORK TO SEE?
 DID HE SMILE HIS WORK TO SEE?

 A dawn and a dusk,
 A night and a day,
 A winter and a spring,
  DID HE SMILE HIS WORK TO SEE?
  DID HE SMILE HIS WORK TO SEE?

A boy and a girl,
A sinner and a saint,
A king and a pauper,
 DID HE SMILE HIS WORK TO SEE?
 DID HE SMILE HIS WORK TO SEE?

 A dream and a fact,
 A hope and a fear,
 A joy and a sorrow,
  DID HE SMILE HIS WORK TO SEE?
  DID HE SMILE HIS WORK TO SEE?

A Friday and a Sunday,
A desert and a river,
A fool and a sage,
 DID HE SMILE HIS WORK TO SEE?
 DID HE SMILE HIS WORK TO SEE?

 A cellar and an attic,
 A mountain and a valley,
 A birth and a death,
  DID HE SMILE HIS WORK TO SEE?
  DID HE SMILE HIS WORK TO SEE?

PRAYER

Father, giver of all life and good,
  your works bring joy and praise to our lips.
Through Jesus you have created all things and they
  are good, very good.
Smile upon us, your people, and bless the works of our
  hands, the movements of our hearts, and the vision
  of you and ourselves.
Bless all tigers and lambs!

Did he smile his work to see?

QUOTATIONS

The radiant smile with which she spoke to me
Would gladden even one burning at the stake. *(Dante)*[22]

To arrest, for the space of a breath, the hands busy about the work
of the earth, and compel men entranced by the sight of distant
goals to glance for a moment at the surrounding vision of form and
color, of sunshine and shadows; to make them pause for a look, for
a sigh, for a smile — such is the aim, difficult and evanescent, and
reserved only for a very few to achieve. But sometimes, by the
deserving and the fortunate, even that task is accomplished. And
when it is accomplished — behold! — all the truth of life is there: a
moment of vision, a sigh, a smile — and the return to an eternal rest.
(Joseph Conrad)[23]

Old fashioned eyes —
Not easy to surprise! *(Emily Dickinson)*[24]

Even as here on earth, one sometimes sees
Affection in the eyes, when strong enough
So that the soul is wholly rapt by it. *(Dante)*[25]

Spring

MANTRA: **All this juice and all this joy**

SOURCE: Gerard Manley Hopkins, "Spring"

Nothing is so beautiful as spring —
   When weeds, in wheels, shoot long and lovely and lush;
   Thrush's eggs look little low heavens, and thrush
Through the echoing timber does so rinse and wring
The ear, it strikes like lightnings to hear him sing;
   The glassy peartree leaves and blooms, they brush
   The descending blue; that blue is all in a rush
With richness; the racing lambs too have fair their fling.

What is all this juice and all this joy?
   A strain of the earth's sweet being in the beginning
In Eden garden. — Have, get, before it cloy,
   Before it cloud, Christ, lord, and sour with sinning,
Innocent mind and Mayday in girl and boy,
   Most, O maid's child, thy choice and worthy the winning.[26]

PARALLEL REFERENCES

Yahweh God planted a garden in Eden which is in the east, and
there he put the man he had fashioned. Yahweh God caused to
spring up from the soil every kind of tree, enticing to look at and
good to eat, with the tree of life and the tree of the knowledge of
good and evil in the middle of the garden. A river flowed from
Eden to water the garden, and from there it divided to make four
streams. *(Genesis 2:8-10)*

In the evening of that same day, the first day of the week, the doors
were closed in the room where the disciples were, for fear of the
Jews. Jesus came and stood among them. He said to them, "Peace

be with you," and showed them his hands and his side. The disciples were filled with joy when they saw the Lord, and he said to them again, "Peace be with you." *(John 20:19-21)*

I have come
so that they may have life
and have it to the full. *(John 10:10)*

All this juice and all   this joy

INWARD JOURNEY

ALL THIS JUICE AND ALL THIS JOY,
ALL THIS JUICE AND ALL THIS JOY.
  The juice of rivers overflowing,
  The juice of tears never knowing,
  The juice of dew May sowing.

ALL THIS JUICE AND ALL THIS JOY,
ALL THIS JUICE AND ALL THIS JOY.
  The juice of ideas — mc^2,
  The juice of an argument — free of lairs,
  The juice of insight — intuitively bared.

ALL THIS JUICE AND ALL THIS JOY,
ALL THIS JUICE AND ALL THIS JOY.
  The juice of the Father — creation given,
  The juice of the Son — incarnation driven,
  The juice of the Spirit — Pentecost hidden.

ALL THIS JUICE AND ALL THIS JOY,
ALL THIS JUICE AND ALL THIS JOY.
  The joy of touch at early dawn,
  The joy of sight — a spring fawn,
  The joy of smell — new-mown lawn.

ALL THIS JUICE AND ALL THIS JOY,
ALL THIS JUICE AND ALL THIS JOY.
  The joy of an essay — ordered and right,
  The joy of new truth — direct and light,
  The joy of perception — clear and bright.

ALL THIS JUICE AND ALL THIS JOY,
ALL THIS JUICE AND ALL THIS JOY.
  The joy of sonship — alleluia.
  The joy of brotherhood — alleluia.
  The joy of fellowship — alleluia.

All this juice and all   this joy

PRAYER

Gracious and holy Father,
you who made the orange and the lemon,
you who call us to joy and peace,
help us to be sensitive to your flowing life in all things
and to rejoice in your creative presence and love.
May you be praised and thanked forever. Amen.

QUOTATIONS

Let me tell it my way. One cannot come into possession of joy and keep secrets. *(Jean Montaurier)*[27]

In truth, between my wonder and my joy,
I felt no wish to listen or to speak. *(Dante)*[28]

The mind feeds on that in which it finds joy. *(St. Augustine)*[29]

For it was a spiritual joy; my soul knew that here was a soul that would understand and be in harmony with mine. . . .
                                              (St. Teresa of Avila)[30]

'Tis curious that we only believe as deeply as we live.
                                              (Ralph Waldo Emerson)[31]

Old Woody's face turned upward, his spirit danced and was warmed out among the stars, while his body remained with us and was warmed by the old tin-can brazier. "Never let anyone rob you of your right to be complete. The daylight is for the brain and the senses, the darkness for the heart and the wits. Never, never be afraid. Your brain may fail you one day, but your heart won't." He returned like a comet, leaving behind a shining trail of love. *(Fynn)*[32]

Fellowship

MANTRA: **May I run, rise, rest with Thee**

SOURCE: George Herbert, "Trinity Sunday"

Lord, who hast form'd me out of mud,
And hast redeem'd me through Thy blood,
And sanctified me to do good;

Purge all my sins done heretofore;
For I confess my heavy score,
And I will strive to sin no more.

Enrich my heart, mouth, hands, in me,
With faith, with hope, with charity:
That I may run, rise, rest with Thee.[33]

PARALLEL REFERENCES

Go, therefore, make disciples of all the nations; baptize them in the name of the Father and of the Son and of the Holy Spirit, and teach them to observe all the commands I gave you. And know that I am with you always; yes, to the end of time. *(Matthew 28:19-20)*

So Peter set out with the other disciple to go to the tomb. They ran together, but the other disciple, running faster than Peter, reached the tomb first; he bent down and saw the linen cloths lying on the ground, but did not go in. Simon Peter who was following now came up, went right into the tomb, saw the linen cloths on the ground, and also the cloth that had been over his head; this was not with the linen cloths but rolled up in a place by itself. Then the other disciple who had reached the tomb first also went in; he saw and he believed. *(John 20:3-9)*

When daylight came he left the house and made his way to a lonely place. The crowds went to look for him . . . . *(Luke 4:42)*

Now about eight days after this had been said, he took with him Peter and John and James and went up the mountain to pray.
(Luke 9:28)

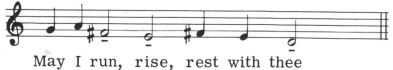

May I run, rise, rest with thee

INWARD JOURNEY

MAY I RUN, RISE, REST WITH THEE.
MAY I RUN, RISE, REST WITH THEE.
   To run: "down the nights and down the days"
      from Emmaus to Jerusalem,
      the good and only race.

MAY I RUN, RISE, REST WITH THEE.
MAY I RUN, RISE, REST WITH THEE.
   To rise: from valleyed betrayals
      from stoneless accusations
      from arrogant doubt.

MAY I RUN, RISE, REST WITH THEE.
MAY I RUN, RISE, REST WITH THEE.
   To rest: "our hearts are restless"
      "with repining restlessness"
      "come to the waters"

MAY I RUN, RISE, REST WITH THEE.
MAY I RUN, RISE, REST WITH THEE.
   Francis I caught, weary.
   Clopas I enflamed, despondent.
   Paul I goaded, zealous.

MAY I RUN, RISE, REST WITH THEE.
MAY I RUN, RISE, REST WITH THEE.
   Peter I beheld, despairing.
   Mary I forgave, unfaithful.
   Thomas I touched, lost.

MAY I RUN, RISE, REST WITH THEE.
MAY I RUN, RISE, REST WITH THEE.
   Augustine I consoled, weary.
   Herbert I nourished, famished.
   Isaiah I filled, empty.

May I run, rise, rest with thee

PRAYER

Lord God,
in Jesus your Son you have walked our earth,
  risen to new life, and rested in peace and love.
Send your Spirit into our hearts that we too
  might live the life of Jesus.
Grant the snail-ness of our steps your speed,
  the valley-ness of our moods your mountain peaks,
    the troubled waters of our journey your calmness.
May your Spirit guide us in your ways. Amen.

QUOTATIONS

Those who are enjoying something, or suffering something together are companions. Those who enjoy or suffer one another, are not. *(C. S. Lewis)*[34]

Every man goes through life shielding his individual smallness behind a majestic group of giants whom he chooses as life companions. This august and mighty troupe is acquired sometimes all at once, sometimes in the course of years. The choice of such peerless companions is made because their personality charms us, their life inspires us, or their word enlightens us. Sometimes we have had the good fortune to know them personally; more often we come to know them through their work, their speeches, writings, thoughts, and example. But maybe it is not we who choose them to accompany us on life's journey; maybe it is they who from their exalted place reach down to adopt us, even as the sun in its journey across the heavens chooses to mirror itself in the humble water of a brooklet. *(Félix Martí-Ibáñez)*[35]

Both messenger and friend of Christ he proved. *(Dante)*[36]

. . . My mariners,
Souls that have toiled, and wrought, and thought with me —
                                        (Alfred Lord Tennyson)[37]

It [friendship] is fit for serene days and graceful gifts and country rambles, but also for rough roads and hard fare, shipwreck, poverty and persecution. *(Ralph Waldo Emerson)*[38]

Presence

MANTRA: **Live through love in his presence**

SOURCE: Ephesians 1:3-12

Blessed be God the Father of our Lord Jesus Christ,
who has blessed us with all the spiritual blessings of heaven
   in Christ.
Before the world was made, he chose us, chose us in Christ,
to be holy and spotless, and to live through love in his presence,
determining that we should become his adopted sons, through
   Jesus Christ
for his own kind purposes,
to make us praise the glory of his grace,
his free gift to us in the Beloved,
in whom, through his blood, we gain our freedom, the
   forgiveness of our sins.
Such is the richness of the grace
which he has showered on us
in all wisdom and insight.
He has let us know the mystery of his purpose,
the hidden plan he so kindly made in Christ from the beginning
to act upon when the times had run their course to the end:
that he would bring everything together under Christ, as head,
everything in the heavens and everything on earth.
And it is in him that we were claimed as God's own,
chosen from the beginning,
under the predetermined plan of the one who guides all things
as he decides by his own will;
chosen to be,
for his greater glory,
the people who would put their hopes in Christ before he came.

PARALLEL REFERENCES

If anyone loves me he will keep my word,
and my Father will love him,
and we shall come to him
and make our home with him. *(John 14:23)*

And under his eyes I have found true peace. *(Song of Songs 8:9-10)*

For I am certain of this: neither death nor life, no angel, no prince,
nothing that exists, nothing still to come, not any power, or height
or depth, nor any created thing, can ever come between us and the
love of God made visible in Christ Jesus our Lord. *(Romans 8:38-39)*

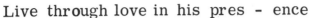

Live through love in his pres - ence

INWARD JOURNEY

> LIVE THROUGH LOVE IN HIS PRESENCE,
> LIVE THROUGH LOVE IN HIS PRESENCE.
>> Live life not death,
>>> light not darkness,
>>> peace not war.

> LIVE THROUGH LOVE IN HIS PRESENCE,
> LIVE THROUGH LOVE IN HIS PRESENCE.
>> Love the great and the small,
>>> the spring and the fall,
>>> the Lord of us all.

> LIVE THROUGH LOVE IN HIS PRESENCE,
> LIVE THROUGH LOVE IN HIS PRESENCE.
>> In intimacy and hopes,
>>> courtroom and ropes,
>>> music and slopes.

Moses, chosen leader,
John, beloved evangelist,
Gandhi, gentle warrior,
> LIVED THROUGH LOVE IN MY PRESENCE,
> LIVED THROUGH LOVE IN MY PRESENCE.

Coleridge's weddingless mariner,
Hopkins' grieving Margaret,
Yahweh's beloved son,
> LIVED THROUGH LOVE IN MY PRESENCE,
> LIVED THROUGH LOVE IN MY PRESENCE.

Blake's little black boy,
Henry's principled chancellor,
John's Carmel pilgrims,
> LIVED THROUGH LOVE IN MY PRESENCE,
> LIVED THROUGH LOVE IN MY PRESENCE.

PRAYER

Loving Father,
your call is simple and profound.
We are to live, and live to the full;
  we are to love unto death;
    we are to dwell in your grace and power.
Enable us to answer your call and to bring you
  glory and praise. Amen.

QUOTATIONS

. . . and she [Monica] had you as her inward teacher in the school
of her heart. . . . Whosoever among them knew her greatly
praised you, and honored you and loved you in her, because they
recognized your presence in her heart, for the fruit of her holy life
bore witness to this. *(St. Augustine)*[39]

Where she is present all others will be more than they are wont . . .
believing, as she did, that by dealing nobly with all, all would show
themselves noble. *(Ralph Waldo Emerson)*[40]

Bodily presence of another is the presence of the incarnate spirit of
the other; and that incarnate spirit reveals itself to me by every shift
of eyes, countenance, color, lips, voice, tone, fingers, hands, arms,
stance. Such revelation is not an object to be apprehended. Rather
it works immediately upon my subjectivity, to make me share the
other's seriousness or vivacity, ease or embarrassment, joy or sorrow; and similarly my response affects his subjectivity, leads him to
say more, or quietly and imperceptibly rebuffs him, holds him off,
closes the door. *(Bernard Lonergan)*[41]

If affinity limits, it also commits — as love always does. *(Walter Kerr)*[42]

The work of love not only heals the roots of sin, but nurtures practical goodness. When it is authentic you will be sensitive to every
need and respond with a generosity unspoiled by selfish intent.
Anything you attempt to do without this love will certainly be im-
perfect, for it is sure to be marred by ulterior motives.
(The Cloud of Unknowing)[43]

Priority

MANTRA: **Your love is better than life**

SOURCE: Psalm 63

God, you are my God, I am seeking you,
my soul is thirsting for you,
my flesh is longing for you,
a land parched, weary and waterless;
I long to gaze on you in the Sanctuary,
and to see your power and glory.

Your love is better than life itself,
my lips will recite your praise;
all my life I will bless you,
in your name lift up my hands;
my soul will feast most richly,
on my lips a song of joy and, in my mouth, praise.

On my bed I think of you,
I meditate on you all night long,
for you have always helped me.
I sing for joy in the shadow of your wings;
my soul clings close to you,
your right hand supports me.

But may those now hounding me to death
go down to the earth below,
consigned to the edge of the sword,
and left as food for jackals.
Then will the king rejoice in God,
and all who swear by him be able to boast
once these lying mouths are silenced.

PARALLEL REFERENCES

Then Jesus said to the Twelve, "What about you, do you want to go away too?" Simon Peter answered, "Lord, who shall we go to? You have the message of eternal life, and we believe; we know that you are the Holy One of God." *(John 6:67-69)*

Then he withdrew from them, about a stone's throw away, and knelt down and prayed. "Father," he said, "if you are willing, take this cup away from me. Nevertheless, let your will be done, not mine." *(Luke 22:41-42)*

Your love is bet-ter than life

INWARD JOURNEY

> YOUR LOVE IS BETTER THAN LIFE.
> YOUR LOVE IS BETTER THAN LIFE.
> Words without compassion . . .
> Deeds without gentleness . . .
> Thoughts without gladness . . .
> Desolation!

> YOUR LOVE IS BETTER THAN LIFE.
> YOUR LOVE IS BETTER THAN LIFE.
> Gifts without cheer . . .
> Talents without sharing . . .
> Riches without peace . . .
> Division!

> YOUR LOVE IS BETTER THAN LIFE.
> YOUR LOVE IS BETTER THAN LIFE.
> Life without love . . .
> Existence without tenderness . . .
> Years without tears . . .
> Death!

YOUR LOVE IS BETTER THAN LIFE.
YOUR LOVE IS BETTER THAN LIFE.
Your compassionate silence . . .
Your gentle nudgings . . .
Your grace-filled plan . . .
Joy!

YOUR LOVE IS BETTER THAN LIFE.
YOUR LOVE IS BETTER THAN LIFE.
Your gift in Eucharist . . .
Your call to share . . .
Your wealth of concern . . .
Union!

YOUR LOVE IS BETTER THAN LIFE.
YOUR LOVE IS BETTER THAN LIFE.
Your living in love . . .
Your reaching out in hope . . .
Your sharing our death . . .
Eternal life!

Your love is bet - ter than life

PRAYER OF THE LOG

Lord, I sit before your burning fire, not alive yet not quite consumed. My brothers and sisters tell me that your love is better than life as they gave themselves to you in joyful immolation. Can I not have my own life and your love? Must I, too, go to fire? Lord, answer and help me.

QUOTATIONS

Sir, I love you more than word can wield the matter;
Dearer than eyesight, space, and liberty;
Beyond what can be valued, rich or rare;
No less than life, with grace, health, beauty, honor;

As much as child e'er loved, or father found;
A love that makes breath poor, and speech unable.
Beyond all manner of so much I love you. *(Shakespeare)*[44]

(In Robert Bolt's *A Man for All Seasons,* Margaret, the daughter of
Sir Thomas More, tries to argue with her father that his approaching death need not be.)

Margaret: But in reason! Haven't you done as much as God can
reasonably *want?*
More: Well . . . finally . . . it isn't a matter of reason; finally
it's a matter of love.[45]

Death is better for every eorl
Than life besmirched with the brand of shame. *(Beowulf)*[46]

Beloved

MANTRA: **You are precious in my eyes**

SOURCE: Isaiah 43:1-5

But now, thus says Yahweh,
who created you, Jacob,
who formed you, Israel:

Do not be afraid, for I have redeemed you;
I have called you by your name, you are mine.
Should you pass through the sea, I will be with you;
or through rivers, they will not swallow you up.
Should you walk through fire, you will not be scorched
and the flames will not burn you.
For I am Yahweh, your God,
the Holy One of Israel, your savior.

I give Egypt for your ransom,
and exchange Cush and Seba for you.
Because you are precious in my eyes,
because you are honored and I love you,
I give men in exchange for you,
people in return for your life.
Do not be afraid, for I am with you.

PARALLEL REFERENCES

As Jesus was walking on from there he saw a man named Matthew sitting by the customs house, and he said to him, "Follow me." And he got up and followed him. *(Matthew 9:9)*

When Jesus reached the spot he looked up and spoke to him: "Zacchaeus, come down. Hurry, because I must stay at your house today." And he hurried down and welcomed him joyfully.

(Luke 19:5-6)

And he [the rich young man] said to him, "Master, I have kept all these from my earliest days." Jesus looked steadily at him and loved him, and he said, "There is one thing you lack. Go and sell everything you own and give the money to the poor, and you will have treasure in heaven; then come, follow me." *(Mark 10:20-21)*

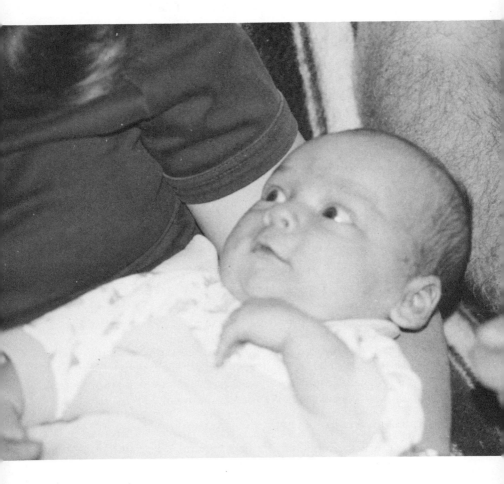

You are pre - cious in my eyes

INWARD JOURNEY

YOU ARE PRECIOUS IN MY EYES,
YOU ARE PRECIOUS IN MY EYES.
    I see your heart, what is and what can be,
    I see your thoughts, those distant and near,
    I see your deeds, life-giving and death-filled.

YOU ARE PRECIOUS IN MY EYES,
YOU ARE PRECIOUS IN MY EYES.
    I long to share my love with you,
    I yearn each moment my peace to give,
    I ponder your plight with deep concern.

YOU ARE PRECIOUS IN MY EYES,
YOU ARE PRECIOUS IN MY EYES.
    I am a God of love and peace,
    I am the Lord of space and time,
    I am your friend, come dwell with me.

You are pre - cious in my eyes

PRAYER

Lord, may we always live in your sight, sensing your tender, compassionate love. You are courteous and familiar; may we love you
as you love us. We praise you in Jesus, who made visible your gaze,
who enfleshed your love. We thank you in your Spirit.

QUOTATIONS

Even as here on earth, one sometimes sees
Affection in the eyes, when strong enough
So that the soul is wholly rapt by it. *(Dante)*[47]

There are various ways of being seen. The seeing eye does not
merely reflect what it sees, it also acts upon it. Seeing is a creative
activity. Seeing influences what it sees.

A man can look at another with a look that hardens the other's heart. A man can look at another with curiosity, with lust or malice, with a look that hurts and destroys, with a look that forces the other to resist. A man can look at another with cold indifference, humiliating and degrading the other. A man can also look at another with reverence, and when that happens the other will be given freedom and opportunity to be himself. A man can look at another with kindness and goodness, with a look that encourages and loves, that opens up what is locked up inside the other, that awakens his powers and brings him to himself. *(Romano Guardini)*[48]

This way of looking is first of all attentive. The soul empties itself of all its own contents in order to receive into itself the being it is looking at, just as he is, in all his truth. *(Simone Weil)*[49]

For in the presence of those radiant beams
One is so changed. *(Dante)*[50]

Intimacy

MANTRA: **Since he clings to me in love**

SOURCE: Psalm 91

He who dwells in the shelter of the Most High
and abides in the shade of the Almighty
says to the Lord: "My refuge,
my stronghold, my God in whom I trust!"

It is he who will free you from the snare
of the fowler who seeks to destroy you;
he will conceal you with his pinions
and under his wings you will find refuge.

You will not fear the terror of the night
nor the arrow that flies by day,
nor the plague that prowls in the darkness
nor the scourge that lays waste at noon.

A thousand may fall at your side,
ten thousand fall at your right,
you, it will never approach;
his faithfulness is buckler and shield.

Your eyes have only to look
to see how the wicked are repaid,
you who have said: "Lord, my refuge!"
and have made the Most High your dwelling.

Upon you no evil shall fall,
no plague approach where you dwell.
For you has he commanded his angels,
to keep you in all your ways.

They shall bear you upon their hands
lest you strike your foot against a stone.
On the lion and the viper you will tread
and trample the young lion and the dragon.

Since he clings to me in love, I will free him;
protect him for he knows my name.
When he calls I shall answer: "I am with you."
I will save him in distress and give him glory.

With length of life I will content him;
I shall let him see my saving power.

PARALLEL REFERENCES

Jesus said to her, "Do not cling to me, because I have not yet
ascended to the Father. But go and find the brothers, and tell them:
I am ascending to my Father and your Father, to my God and your
God." So Mary of Magdala went and told the disciples that she had
seen the Lord and that he had said these things to her. *(John 20:17-18)*

She waited behind him at his feet, weeping, and her tears fell on his
feet, and she wiped them away with her hair; then she covered his
feet with kisses and anointed them with the ointment. *(Luke 7:38)*

Since he clings to me in love

INWARD JOURNEY

SINCE HE CLINGS TO ME IN LOVE,
SINCE HE CLINGS TO ME IN LOVE,
    I will honor and esteem my creature,
    I will love and cherish him,
    I will rejoice and acclaim him.

SINCE HE CLINGS TO ME IN LOVE,
SINCE HE CLINGS TO ME IN LOVE,
    My home will be his palace,
    My heart will be his dwelling,
    My family will be his people.

SINCE HE CLINGS TO ME IN LOVE,
SINCE HE CLINGS TO ME IN LOVE,
My pain will be embraced,
My work will generously be done,
My kingdom will powerfully come.

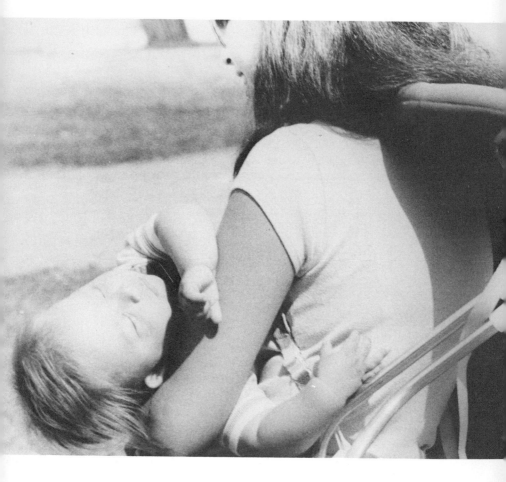

Since he clings to me in love

PRAYER

Lord, we cling to you in love. You are our Father and we love you. "Never let us be parted from you," for in that would be our death. Gift us continually with your love and we shall serve you in whatever you ask. May we cling to you as you cling to us.

QUOTATIONS

Love bade me welcome; yet my soul drew back,
      Guilty of dust and sin.
But quick-eyed Love, observing me grow slack
      From my first entrance in,
Drew nearer to me, sweetly questioning
      If I lack'd anything.

A quest, I answer'd, worthy to be here:
      Love said, You shall be he
I, the unkind, ungrateful? Ah, my dear,
      I cannot look on thee.
Love took my hand, and smiling did reply,
      Who made the eyes but I?

Truth, Lord, but I have marr'd them: let my shame
      Go where it doth deserve.
And know you not, says Love, who bore the blame?
      My dear, then I will serve.
You must sit down, says Love and taste my meat
      So I did sit and eat. *(George Herbert)*[51]

Love was looking into the eyes of the other, and forgetting the dark void between you and forgetting that no one can walk in a void, you start manfully across, your arms outstretched to give of yourself and to receive of the other. *(Murray Bodo)*[52]

I would not give much for that love which is never extravagant, which always observes the proprieties. . . . What mother, what husband or wife, what youth or maiden in love, but says a thousand foolish things, in a way of endearment, which the speaker would be sorry for strangers to hear; yet they are not on that account unwelcome to the parties to whom they are addressed.

(Cardinal Newman)[53]

The love of our neighbor in all its fullness simply means being able to say to him: "What are you going through?" *(Simone Weil)*[54]

The Pulley

MANTRA: **Let him be rich and weary**

SOURCE: George Herbert, "The Pulley"

When God at first made man,
Having a glass of blessing standing by,
Let us, said He, pour on him all we can:
Let the world's riches, which dispersed lie,
  Contract into a span.

So strength first made a way;
Then beauty flow'd; then wisdom, honor, pleasure:
When almost all was out, God made a stay,
Perceiving that alone, of all His treasure,
  Rest in the bottom lay.

For if I should, said He,
Bestow this jewel also on My creature,
He would adore My gifts instead of Me,
And rest in nature, not the God of nature:
  So both should losers be.

Yet let him keep the rest,
But keep them with repining restlessness:
Let him be rich and weary, that at least,
If goodness lead him not, yet weariness
  May toss him to My breast.

PARALLEL REFERENCES

What do you have that was not given to you? And if it was given,
how can you boast as though it were not? *(1 Corinthians 4:7)*

Oh, come to the water all you who are thirsty;
though you have no money, come!
Buy corn without money, and eat,
and, at no cost, wine and milk.
Why spend money on what is not bread,
your wages on what fails to satisfy?
Listen, listen to me, and you will have good things to eat
and rich food to enjoy.
Pay attention, come to me;
listen, and your soul will live. *(Isaiah 55:1-3)*

Come to me, all you who labor and are overburdened, and I will
give you rest. *(Matthew 11:28)*

Let him be rich and wea - ry

INWARD JOURNEY

LET HIM BE RICH AND WEARY,
LET HIM BE RICH AND WEARY,
  In winter's frigid dreams and distant hope,
  In spring's awakening to newness of life,
  In summer's drought and autumn's harvest.

LET HIM BE RICH AND WEARY,
LET HIM BE RICH AND WEARY,
  With friends, time precipitous speed
  With foe and dentist, pain interminable,
  With acquaintances, partings inevitable.

LET HIM BE RICH AND WEARY,
LET HIM BE RICH AND WEARY,
  At parties anticipated, yet not so fun,
  At wakes where consolation touches the heart,
  At beaches that raise eternal questions.

LET HIM BE RICH AND WEARY,
LET HIM BE RICH AND WEARY,
  By mountains majestic and eternally poised,
  By rapids laughing and shining with beauty,
  By forest too "lovely, dark and deep."

Let him be rich and wea - ry

PRAYER

Lord, you gifted us with all good things. Yet we are not satisfied, our winters and springs filled with discontent. Only you can quiet our longings. Only you can take away our weariness and give the wealth of resting in your peace. We thank you in Jesus' name.

QUOTATIONS

What a strange thing! In filling myself, I had emptied myself. In grasping things, I had lost everything. In devouring pleasures and joys, I had found distress and anguish and fear. *(Thomas Merton)*[56]

All which I took from thee I did but take,
    Not for thy harms,
But just that thou might'st seek it in My arms.
    All which thy child's mistake
Fancies as lost, I have stored for thee at home:
    Rise, clasp My hand, and come! *(Francis Thompson)*[57]

But yet, Lord, thanks must be given to you, our God, the most excellent and best creator and ruler of the universe, even if you had willed only to bring me to childhood. Even then I existed, had life and feeling, had care for my own well-being, which is a trace of your own most mysterious unity from which I took my being. By my inner sense I guarded the integrity of my outer senses, and I delighted in truth, in these little things and in thoughts about these little things. I did not want to err; I was endowed with a strong memory; I was well instructed in speech; I was refined by friendship. I shunned sadness, dejection, and ignorance. What was there that was not wonderful and praiseworthy in such a living being?

All these things are the gifts of my God: I did not give them to myself. *(St. Augustine)*[58]

If you're approaching Him [God] not as the goal but as a road, not as the end but as a means, you're not really approaching Him at all.
(C. S. Lewis)[59]

Waiting

MANTRA: **I am standing at the door**

SOURCE: Revelation 3:14-22

Write to the angel of the church in Laodicea and say, "Here is the message of the Amen, the faithful, the true witness, the ultimate source of God's creation: I know all about you: how you are neither cold nor hot. I wish you were one or the other, but since you are neither, but only lukewarm, I will spit you out of my mouth. You say to yourself, 'I am rich, I have made a fortune, and have everything I want,' never realizing that you are wretchedly and pitiably poor, and blind and naked too. I warn you, buy from me the gold that has been tested in the fire to make you really rich, and white robes to clothe you and cover your shameful nakedness, and eye ointment to put on your eyes so that you are able to see. I am the one who reproves and disciplines all those he loves: so repent in real earnest. Look, I am standing at the door, knocking. If one of you hears me calling and opens the door, I will come in to share his meal, side by side with him. Those who prove victorious I will allow to share my throne, just as I was victorious myself and took my place with my Father on his throne. If anyone has ears to hear, let him listen to what the Spirit is saying to the churches."

PARALLEL REFERENCES

Leaving the synagogue he went to Simon's house. Now Simon's mother-in-law was suffering from a high fever and they asked him to do something for her. Leaning over her he rebuked the fever and it left her. And she immediately got up and began to wait on them.
(Luke 4:38-39)

Do not let your hearts be troubled.
Trust in God still, and trust in me.

There are many rooms in my Father's house;
if there were not, I should have told you.
I am going now to prepare a place for you,
and after I have gone and prepared you a place,
I shall return to take you with me;
so that where I am
you may be too.
You know the way to the place where I am going. *(John 14:1-4)*

All day long I hope in you
because of your goodness, Yahweh. *(Psalm 25:7c)*

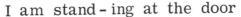

I am stand - ing at the door

INWARD JOURNEY

I AM STANDING AT THE DOOR,
I AM STANDING AT THE DOOR.
   Look into my eyes,
   Gaze into my heart,
   See my tender love.

I AM STANDING AT THE DOOR,
I AM STANDING AT THE DOOR.
   Hoping for a gracious greeting,
   Longing for a warm embrace,
   Yearning welcome . . . no exit.

I AM STANDING AT THE DOOR,
I AM STANDING AT THE DOOR.
   Knocking without forcing,
   Rapping gently, tapping,
   Knuckles raw and sore.

I AM STANDING AT THE DOOR,
I AM STANDING AT THE DOOR.
   Table talk in rich exchange,
   Table food . . . incarnate love.
   Table joy of companions.

I AM STANDING AT THE DOOR,
I AM STANDING AT THE DOOR.
   Calling out of love,
   Pleading to bring life,
   Shouting in gentle whispers.

I AM STANDING AT THE DOOR,
I AM STANDING AT THE DOOR.
   Side by side . . . can it be!
   With-ness . . . deep intimacy.
   Wit-ness . . . hospitality.

PRAYER

Lord, our homes are small and dark. Yet you desire to come and make them your dwelling. For this we praise and thank you. Grace us with hospitality; enable us to hear your call and to quickly respond to your every coming. May we share all with you, and in being with you, may we go forth to witness what you are to us. We ask this in Jesus' name. Amen.

QUOTATIONS

Then came the worst part, the waiting. *(C. S. Lewis)*[60]

The moment before acting may be, as can easily be imagined, peculiarly dreary — the mind may be confused — no reason for acting may be forthcoming in our mind — and the awful greatness of the step in itself, and without any distinct apprehension of its consequences, may weigh on us. Some persons like to be left to themselves in such a crisis — others find comfort in the presence of others — I could do nothing but shut myself in my room and lie down on my bed. *(Cardinal Newman)*[61]

It was late. I did not have many hours to sleep, and I did not sleep much. I felt something that was not only fear, though I felt fear too. What I felt was what we see in the eye of a bird or an animal that we are about to kill, which knows that it is about to be killed, and whose torment is not the certainty of death or pain, but the horror of the interval before death comes, in which it knows that it has lost light and freedom forever. It is not yet dead. But it is no longer alive. *(Whittaker Chambers)*[62]

As he could not avoid the danger, he hurried to meet it, for these seconds of uncertainty had already become so painful to him that all he longed for was to cut them short. *(Alessandro Manzoni)*[63]

Grow old along with me!
The best is yet to be,
The last of life, for which the first was made.
Our times are in his hand
Who saith, "A whole I planned;
Youth shows but half. Trust God; see all, nor be afraid!"
                                    (Robert Browning)[64]

Life

SOURCE: John 10:1-10

Jesus said:
"Truly I assure you:
Whoever does not enter the sheepfold
    through the gate but climbs in some other way
is a thief and a marauder.
The one who enters through the gate
is shepherd of the sheep;
the keeper opens the gate for him.
The sheep hear his voice
as he calls his own by name
and leads them out.
When he has brought out all those that are his,
he walks in front of them,
and the sheep follow him
because they recognize his voice.
They will not follow a stranger;
such a one they will flee,
because they do not recognize a stranger's voice."

Even though Jesus used this figure with them, they did not grasp what he was trying to tell them. He therefore said to them again:

"My solemn word is this:
I am the sheepgate.
All who came before me
were thieves and marauders
whom the sheep did not heed.
I am the gate.
Whoever enters through me
will be safe.
He will go in and out,
and find pasture.

The thief comes
only to steal and slaughter and destroy.
I came that they might have life
and have it to the full."

PARALLEL REFERENCES

I have been crucified with Christ, and I live now not with my own
life but with the life of Christ who lives in me. The life I now live in
this body I live in faith: faith in the Son of God who loved me and
who sacrificed himself for my sake. *(Galatians 2:19-20)*

This is the testimony:
God has given us eternal life
and this life is in his Son;
anyone who has the Son has life,
anyone who does not have the Son does not have life.

(1 John 5:11-12)

I came that they may   have life

INWARD JOURNEY

I CAME THAT THEY MAY HAVE LIFE,
I CAME THAT THEY MAY HAVE LIFE.
To Mary I came to receive and give life,
To Elizabeth I came to make her heart rejoice,
To Joseph I came to help and be helped.

I CAME THAT THEY MAY HAVE LIFE,
I CAME THAT THEY MAY HAVE LIFE.
To the Jordan I came to be with the crowd,
To the synagogue I came to worship my Father,
To the hovels I came to mend mind and body.

I CAME THAT THEY MAY HAVE LIFE,
I CAME THAT THEY MAY HAVE LIFE.
To the lakes I came looking for help,
To the hills I came for peace and solitude,
To the table I came to be fed and to feed.

I CAME THAT THEY MAY HAVE LIFE,
I CAME THAT THEY MAY HAVE LIFE.
To the cross I came as my Father asked,
To the grave I came to conquer sin and death,
To the upper room I came with joy and peace.

I came that they may   have life

PRAYER

Lord, you are the author of life and love. You came to reconcile us
to your Father, to fill us with your grace, to challenge us to work

with you in building the Kingdom. May your Spirit transmit life through us; may we be channels and instruments of your love to others. We pray this in simple faith and trust. Amen.

QUOTATIONS

Fear not that life should come to an end, but rather that it should never have a beginning. *(Cardinal Newman)*[65]

Life enjoys, abstains from, suffers, struggles, creates. It enfolds and permeates things, joins with other life, resulting not in a mere sum, but in new and manifold vitality. Foremost and fundamental, it is and remains an inexplicable enigma. For is it not strange that in order to possess one thing we must relinquish another? That in order to do anything of genuine value we must focus our attention on it and away from all else? That when we wish to do justice to one person we do injustice to all others, if only by not likewise accepting them into our range of heart, simply because there is not room enough for everyone? That when we experience any powerful sensation, then only in ignorance of what it is, the instant we try to understand it, the current is cut? *(Romano Guardini)*[66]

Our task is always the humble and courageous one of listening obediently and acting boldly. *(Romano Guardini)*[67]

If we live truly, we shall see truly. *(Ralph Waldo Emerson)*[68]

Simplicity

MANTRA: **One thing I ask of the Lord**

SOURCE: Psalm 27:1-5

The Lord is my light and my help;
whom shall I fear?
The Lord is the stronghold of my life;
before whom shall I shrink?

When evil-doers draw near
to devour my flesh,
it is they, my enemies and foes,
who stumble and fall.

Though an army encamp against me
my heart would not fear.
Though war break out against me
even then would I trust.

There is one thing I ask of the Lord,
for this I long,
to live in the house of the Lord
all the days of my life,
to savor the sweetness of the Lord,
to behold his temple.

For there he keeps me safe in his tent
in the day of evil.
He hides me in the shelter of his tent,
on a rock he sets me safe.

PARALLEL REFERENCES

It is the pagans of this world who set their hearts on all these things.
Your Father well knows you need them. No; set your hearts on his
kingdom, and these other things will be given you as well.

(Luke 12:30-31)

For I am certain of this: neither death nor life, no angel, no prince,
nothing that exists, nothing still to come, not any power, or height
or depth, nor any created thing, can ever come between us and the
love of God made visible in Christ Jesus our Lord. *(Romans 8:38-39)*

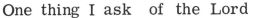

One thing I ask of the Lord

INWARD JOURNEY

ONE THING I ASK OF THE LORD,
ONE THING I ASK OF THE LORD.
  A life free from pain?
  A sky always without a cloud?
  A field emptied of stone?

ONE THING I ASK OF THE LORD,
ONE THING I ASK OF THE LORD.
  Friends who have no faults?
  Toads without warts?
  A child with no freckles?

ONE THING I ASK OF THE LORD,
ONE THING I ASK OF THE LORD.
  All pluses, no minuses?
  All victories, no defeats?
  All success, no failure?

ONE THING I ASK OF THE LORD,
ONE THING I ASK OF THE LORD.
  The ability to say *yes* to what has been!
  The courage to say *amen* to what is!
  The trust to say *alleluia* to what will be!

PRAYER

Lord, there are so many things that seek entrance into our hearts —
so many gifts, so many activities, so many opportunities. Help us
to be simple and poor. Help us to know what is truly pleasing to
you. Lord, gift us with the Spirit of your wisdom.

QUOTATIONS

You lack simplicity when you are far from God. *(Raïssa Maritain)*[69]

Now I see that I was all mixed up, that I had fragmented my life into many sections that did not really form a unity. The question is not, "Do I have time to prepare?" but, "Do I live in a state of preparedness?" When God is my only concern, when God is the center of my interest, when all my prayers, my reading, my studying, my speaking, and writing serve only to know God better and to make him known better, then there is no basis for anxiety or stage fright. Then I can live in such a state of preparedness and trust that speaking from the heart is also speaking to the heart. My fears and my resulting fatigue over the last three years might well be diagnosed as a lack of single-mindedness, as a lack of one-eyedness, as a lack of simplicity. Indeed, how divided my heart has been and still is! I want to love God, but also to make a career. I want to be a good Christian, but also have my successes as a teacher, preacher, or speaker. I want to be close to Christ but also popular and liked by many people. No wonder that living becomes a tiring enterprise. The characteristic of a saint is, to borrow Kierkegaard's words, "To will one thing." Well, I will more than one thing, am double-hearted, double-minded, and have a very divided loyalty.

(Henri Nouwen)[70]

For all her few years, I saw her then as I see her now, the sanest, the most uncluttered, and the most direct of beings. Her ability to ignore the excesses of information, dismiss the useless frill, and uncover the heart of things was truly magical. *(Fynn)*[71]

Simplicity of intention is the principle and the completion of all virtue. *(Raïssa Maritain, quoting Ruysbroeck)*[72]

Confession

MANTRA: **And you have pardoned my sin**

SOURCE: Psalm 32:1-7

Happy the man whose fault is forgiven,
   whose sin is blotted out;
happy the man whom Yahweh
   accuses of no guilt,
   whose spirit is incapable of deceit!

All the time I kept silent, my bones were wasting away
   with groans, day in, day out;
day and night your hand
   lay heavy on me;
my heart grew parched as stubble
   in summer drought.

At last I admitted to you I had sinned;
   no longer concealing my guilt,
I said, "I will go to Yahweh
   and confess my fault."
And you, you have forgiven the wrong I did,
   have pardoned my sin.

That is why each of your servants prays to you
   in time of trouble;
even if floods come rushing down,
   they will never reach him.
You are a hiding place for me,
   you guard me when in trouble,
you surround me with songs of deliverance.

PARALLEL REFERENCES

"For this reason I tell you that her sins, her many sins, must have been forgiven her, or she would not have shown such great love. It is the man who is forgiven little who shows little love." Then he said to her, "Your sins are forgiven." Those who were with him at table began to say to themselves, "Who is this man, that he even forgives sins?" But he said to the woman, "Your faith has saved you; go in peace." *(Luke 7:47-50)*

After saying this he [Jesus] breathed on them and said:
  "Receive the Holy Spirit.
  For those whose sins you forgive,
  they are forgiven;
  for those whose sins you retain,
  they are retained." *(John 20:22-23)*

And you have par - doned my   sin

INWARD JOURNEY

AND YOU HAVE PARDONED MY SIN,
AND YOU HAVE PARDONED MY SIN.
  As a child — in my taking all things for granted,
        in temper tantrums and subtle blackmails,
        in my whining and demanding tears.

AND YOU HAVE PARDONED MY SIN,
AND YOU HAVE PARDONED MY SIN.
  As a youth — in following the crowd, like a leaf in the wind,
        in indulgence to every season's whim,
        in cruel irreverence for nature and man.

AND YOU HAVE PARDONED MY SIN,
AND YOU HAVE PARDONED MY SIN.
  As an adult — in my search for fame and power,
        in my playing God, even with the flowers,
        in my despair and wandering hours.

AND YOU HAVE PARDONED MY SIN,
AND YOU HAVE PARDONED MY SIN.
  As a life's veteran — in my foolish longings for what might
        have been,
        in my resistance to death and clutching
        of life,
        in my harbored resentments and lack
        of forgiveness.

    AND YOU HAVE PARDONED MY SIN,
    AND YOU HAVE PARDONED MY SIN.

And you have par - doned my   sin

PRAYER

Lord, your mercy is boundless, your love extravagant. In every season of life we have turned from your gentle command and attempted to manage our own lives. Now we confess that we have lived in darkness and that you are truly our light; that we have been deaf to your call, a call of intimacy and tenderness. Thank you for your pardon; help us to appreciate the Cross, through which our sins were forgiven.

QUOTATIONS

Christianity tells people to repent and promises them forgiveness. It therefore has nothing (as far as I know) to say to people who do not know they have done anything to repent of and who do not feel that they need any forgiveness. *(C. S. Lewis)*[73]

Into so many and such grave occasions of sin did I fall, and so far was my soul led astray by all these vanities, that I was ashamed to return to God and to approach Him in the intimate friendship which comes from prayer. *(St. Teresa of Avila)*[74]

And mercy is an operation which comes from the goodness of God, and it will go on operating so long as sin is permitted to harass righteous souls. And when sin is no longer permitted to harass, then the operation of mercy will cease. And then all will be brought into righteousness and stand fast there forever. By his toleration we fall, and in his blessed love, with his power and his wisdom, we are protected, and by mercy and grace we are raised to much more joy. And so in righteousness and in mercy he wished to be known and loved, now and forever. And the soul that wisely contemplates in grace is well satisfied with both, and endlessly delights.

(Julian of Norwich)[75]

One hope, one trust, one firm promise — your mercy! *(St. Augustine)*[76]

In the resurrection-experience, which is typified by the apparitions, Jesus does not turn against those who failed to recognize him and put him to death; instead he offers them pardon and invites them to follow his own path. . . . One now realizes that one's own sinfulness is no perduring obstacle to finding meaning in life and fleshing it out in reality. *(Jon Sobrino)*[77]

Praise

MANTRA: **I will praise you for ever**

SOURCE: Psalm 30

High praise, Yahweh, I give you, for you have helped me up,
and not let my enemies gloat over me.
Yahweh, my God, I cried to you for help, and you have
    healed me.
Yahweh, you have brought my soul up from Sheol,
of all those who go down to the Pit you have revived me.

Play music in Yahweh's honor, you devout,
remember his holiness, and praise him.
His anger lasts a moment, his favor a lifetime;
in the evening, a spell of tears, in the morning, shouts of joy.

In my prosperity, I used to say,
"Nothing can ever shake me!"
Your favor, Yahweh, stood me on a peak impregnable;
but then you hid your face and I was terrified.

Yahweh, I call to you,
I beg my God to pity me,
"What do you gain by my blood if I go down to the Pit?
Can the dust praise you or proclaim your faithfulness?

"Hear, Yahweh, take pity on me;
Yahweh, help me!"
You have turned my mourning into dancing,
you have stripped off my sackcloth and wrapped me in gladness;
and now my heart, silent no longer, will play you music;
Yahweh, my God, I will praise you for ever.

PARALLEL REFERENCES

"But to prove to you that the Son of Man has authority on earth to forgive sins," — he said to the paralyzed man — "I order you: get up, and pick up your stretcher and go home." And immediately before their very eyes he got up, picked up what he had been lying on and went home praising God. They were all astounded and praised God, and were filled with awe, saying, "We have seen strange things today." *(Luke 5:24-26)*

My soul proclaims the greatness of the Lord
and my spirit exults in God my savior;
because he has looked upon his lowly handmaid. *(Luke 1:46)*

I will praise you for ev - er

INWARD JOURNEY

I WILL PRAISE YOU FOR EVER,
I WILL PRAISE YOU FOR EVER.
For autumn pumpkins,
June asparagus,
February thaws.

I WILL PRAISE YOU FOR EVER,
I WILL PRAISE YOU FOR EVER.
For hot French fries,
thirst-quenching beer,
wild, hiding strawberries.

I WILL PRAISE YOU FOR EVER,
I WILL PRAISE YOU FOR EVER.
For hope in a forgotten friendship,
courage on blue Mondays,
joy in the midst of sorrow.

I WILL PRAISE YOU FOR EVER,
I WILL PRAISE YOU FOR EVER.
For the touch of a human hand,
the sound of a friend's advice,
the marvel of your love.

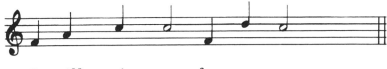

I will praise you for ev - er

PRAYER

Lord Jesus, all praise and thanks be yours. Your coming and living among us have shown forth the Father's love. Your dying and rising have conquered sin and death. Praise to you for ever. Amen! Amen! Alleluia!

QUOTATIONS

You are great, O Lord, and greatly to be praised: great is your power and to your wisdom there is no limit. And man, who is a part of your creation, wishes to praise you, man who bears about within himself his mortality, who bears about within himself testimony to his sin and testimony that you resist the proud. Yet man, this part of your creation, wishes to praise you. You arouse him to take joy in praising you, for you have made us for yourself, and our heart is restless until it rests in you. *(St. Augustine)*[78]

Glory be to God for dappled things —
　　For skies of couple-colour as a brinded cow;
　　　　For rose-moles all in stipple upon trout that swim;
Fresh-firecoal chestnut falls; finches' wings;
　　Landscape plotted and pieced — fold, fallow, and plough;
　　　　And all trades, their gear and tackle and trim.
All things counter, original, spare, strange;
　　Whatever is fickle, freckled (who knows how?)
　　　　With swift, slow; sweet, sour; adazzle, dim;
He fathers-forth whose beauty is past change:
　　　　　　　　Praise him. *(Gerard Manley Hopkins)*[79]

Ah, but some did return: the widow's son,
The girl Jairus loved, and he for whom
Martha and Mary wept! These Jesus won
Back to mortality, snatched from the tomb.
They did come back. But they have left no word
Of that far country to which we must go
Who never will return. What they have seen and heard
Until we reach that bourne we shall not know.

There must have been a strange light in the eyes
Lit by a soul that had seen heaven and God.
For one who had passed the judgment, great surprise
At things that men call good. He must have trod
The earth an alien. Silent he must be
For want of words who has glimpsed eternity. *(Ruth Mary Fox)*[80]

Instrumentality

MANTRA: **In his quiver he hid me**

SOURCE: Isaiah 49:1-6

Hear me, O coastlands,
  listen, O distant peoples.
The Lord called me from birth,
  from my mother's womb he gave me my name.

He made of me a sharp-edged sword
  and concealed me in the shadow of his arm.
He made me a polished arrow,
  in his quiver he hid me.
You are my servant, he said to me,
  Israel, through whom I show my glory.

Though I thought I had toiled in vain,
  and for nothing, uselessly, spent my strength,
Yet my reward is with the Lord,
  my recompense is with my God.
For now the Lord has spoken
  who formed me as his servant from the womb,
That Jacob may be brought back to him
  and Israel gathered to him;
And I am made glorious in the sight of the Lord,
  and my God is now my strength!

It is too little, he says, for you to be my servant,
  to raise up the tribes of Jacob,
  and restore the survivors of Israel;
I will make you a light to the nations,
  that my salvation may reach to the ends of the earth.

PARALLEL REFERENCES

This is how Jesus Christ came to be born. His mother Mary was betrothed to Joseph; but before they came to live together she was found to be with child through the Holy Spirit. *(Matthew 1:18)*

When they had done everything the Law of the Lord required, they went back to Galilee, to their own town of Nazareth. Meanwhile the child grew to maturity, and he was filled with wisdom; and God's favor was with him. *(Luke 2:39-40)*

In his quiv - er he hid me

INWARD JOURNEY

IN HIS QUIVER HE HID ME,
IN HIS QUIVER HE HID ME.
From winds too violent for an inexperienced arrow,
From destinations too remote for a limited messenger,
From untimely use, for a useful time.

IN HIS QUIVER HE HID ME,
IN HIS QUIVER HE HID ME.
Out of love for so humble an instrument,
Out of love for defenseless victims,
Out of love for the arrow-maker.

IN HIS QUIVER HE HID ME,
IN HIS QUIVER HE HID ME.
For the one long, lonely flight,
For the whisper of love that would pierce a soul,
For the journey of no return.

PRAYER

Lord, in your love you protect us, and out of love you send us forth
to build the Kingdom. Nurtured by your care, may we, in freedom,
respond to your sending us forth for whatever task, on whatever
day, to whomever you desire. May your will be done. Amen.

QUOTATIONS

"Be at peace," I told her. And she had knelt to receive this peace.
May she keep it for ever. It will be I that give it her. Oh, miracle—
thus to be able to give what we ourselves do not possess, sweet
miracle—of our empty hands! Hope which was shrivelling in my
heart flowered again in hers; the spirit of prayer which I thought
lost in me for ever was given back to her by God and—who can tell
—perhaps in *my* name! Lord, I am stripped bare of all things, as
you alone can strip us bare, whose fearful care nothing escapes, nor
your terrible love! *(Georges Bernanos)*[81]

. . . there is good reason to think that God was sending you this truth through the pen I am holding. It is more suitable for some thoughts to come by direct inspiration; it is more suitable for others to be transmitted through some creature. *(Simone Weil)*[82]

Lord, make me an instrument of your peace.
Where there is hatred, let me sow love.
Where there is injury, pardon.
Where there is doubt, faith.
Where there is despair, hope.
Where there is darkness, light.
Where there is sadness, joy.

Divine Master, grant that I may not so much seek to be consoled
    as to console,
To be understood as to understand,
To be loved as to love,
For it is in giving that we receive,
It is in pardoning that we are pardoned,
And it is in dying that we are born to eternal life.

(Prayer of St. Francis)

You at your worst are an instrument unstrung: I am an instrument strung but preferring to play itself because it thinks it knows the tune better than the Musician. *(C. S. Lewis)*[83]

Salvation

MANTRA: **For you are God my savior**

SOURCE: Psalm 25:1-11

To you, O Lord, I lift up my soul.
I trust you, let me not be disappointed;
do not let my enemies triumph.
Those who hope in you shall not be disappointed,
but only those who wantonly break faith.

Lord, make me know your ways.
Lord, teach me your paths.
Make me walk in your truth, and teach me:
for you are God my savior.

In you I hope all day long
because of your goodness, O Lord.
Remember your mercy, Lord,
and the love you have shown from of old.
Do not remember the sins of my youth.
In your love remember me.

The Lord is good and upright.
He shows the path to those who stray,
he guides the humble in the right path;
he teaches his way to the poor.

His ways are faithfulness and love
for those who keep his covenant and will.
Lord, for the sake of your name
forgive my guilt; for it is great.

PARALLEL REFERENCES

And the dead man sat up and began to talk, and Jesus gave him to
his mother. Everyone was filled with awe and praised God saying,

"A great prophet has appeared among us; God has visited his people." *(Luke 7:15-16)*

"Rabbuni," the blind man said to him, "Master, let me see again." Jesus said to him, "Go; your faith has saved you." And immediately his sight returned and he followed him along the road.

(Mark 10:51-52)

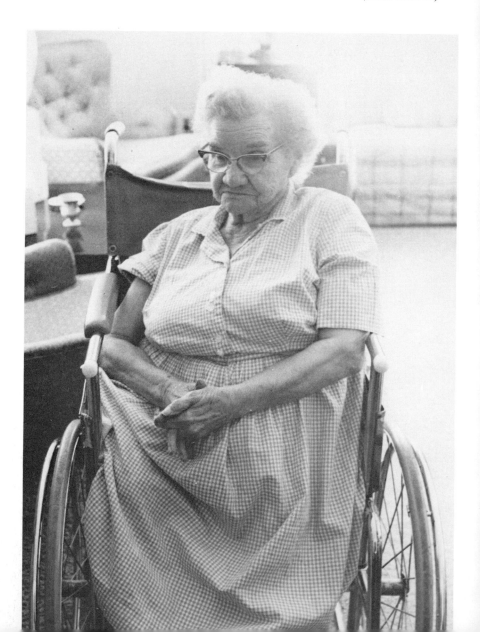

For you are God   my Sav - ior

INWARD JOURNEY

FOR YOU ARE GOD MY SAVIOR,
FOR YOU ARE GOD MY SAVIOR.
  Empty are idols of fame and position,
  Fruitless are deeds not rooted in you,
  Dry and barren are words not nourished at your well.

    FOR YOU ARE GOD MY SAVIOR,
    FOR YOU ARE GOD MY SAVIOR.
      Touching the wounded, the fallen,
      Teaching the barren mind and soul,
      Testing the powerful with weakness.

FOR YOU ARE GOD MY SAVIOR,
FOR YOU ARE GOD MY SAVIOR.
  Delighting in the children of men,
  Rejoicing in tears and laughter,
  Smiling at our frowns and crowns.

    FOR YOU ARE GOD MY SAVIOR,
    FOR YOU ARE GOD MY SAVIOR.
      Bending over the "bent world" bruised,
      Embracing an Anna and Simeon,
      Prodding a Peter and a Paul.

FOR YOU ARE GOD MY SAVIOR,
FOR YOU ARE GOD MY SAVIOR.
  Dying that we might live,
  Rising that we might hope,
  Coming that we might believe.

For you are God   my Sav - ior

PRAYER

God, my savior, you are greater than all things, yet permeate all of life. In every event and person, in every sacrament and word, your presence can be felt and tasted. Be our God, and let us be your people. Save us in your mercy. Amen.

QUOTATIONS

The New Testament makes it clear that reconciliation with God must be understood in an entirely new way on the basis of the cross. Otherwise it might be turned into what Bonhoeffer calls "cheap grace." The reconciliation has cost "blood beyond price" (1 Pet 1:19). Jesus' resurrection does not allow for any nominal reconciliation because one's experience of being reconciled to God must go hand in hand with a realization of its cost. Here we have no magical conception of reconciliation, but a down-to-earth one. There is reconciliation because there was love; and there was love because there was suffering and death. *(Jon Sobrino)*[84]

The Prodigal Son at least walked home on his own feet. But who can duly adore that Love which will open the high gates to a prodigal who is brought in kicking, struggling, resentful, and darting his eyes in every direction for a chance of escape? *(C. S. Lewis)*[85]

But yet, Lord, thanks must be given to you, our God, the most excellent and best creator and ruler of the universe, even if you had willed only to bring me to childhood. Even then I existed, had life and feeling, had care for my own well-being, which is a trace of your own most mysterious unity from which I took my being. By my inner sense I guarded the integrity of my outer senses, and I delighted in truth, in these little things and in thoughts about these little things. I did not want to err; I was endowed with a strong memory; I was well instructed in speech; I was refined by friendship. I shunned sadness, dejection, and ignorance. What was there that was not wonderful and praiseworthy in such a living being?

   All these things are the gifts of my God: I did not give them to myself. *(St. Augustine)*[86]

When God looks, He loves and grants favors. *(St. John of the Cross)*[87]

Words

MANTRA: **Deeply troubled by these words**

SOURCE: Luke 1:26-38

In the sixth month, the angel Gabriel was sent from God to a town of Galilee named Nazareth, to a virgin betrothed to a man named Joseph, of the house of David. The virgin's name was Mary. Upon arriving, the angel said to her: "Rejoice, O highly favored daughter! The Lord is with you. Blessed are you among women." She was deeply troubled by his words, and wondered what his greeting meant. The angel went on to say to her: "Do not fear, Mary. You have found favor with God. You shall conceive and bear a son and give him the name Jesus. Great will be his dignity and he will be called Son of the Most High. The Lord God will give him the throne of David his father. He will rule over the house of Jacob forever and his reign will be without end."

Mary said to the angel, "How can this be since I do not know man?" The angel answered her: "The Holy Spirit will come upon you and the power of the Most High will overshadow you; hence, the holy offspring to be born will be called Son of God. Know that Elizabeth your kinswoman has conceived a son in her old age; she who was thought to be sterile is now in her sixth month, for nothing is impossible with God."

Mary said, "I am the servant of the Lord. Let it be done to me as you say." With that the angel left her.

PARALLEL REFERENCES

Near the cross of Jesus stood his mother and his mother's sister, Mary the wife of Clopas, and Mary of Magdala. Seeing his mother and the disciple he loved standing near her, Jesus said to his mother, "Woman, this is your son." Then to the disciple he said, "This is your mother." And from that moment the disciple made a place for her in his home. *(John 19:25-27)*

Then to all he said, "If anyone wants to be a follower of mine, let him renounce himself and take up his cross every day and follow me. For anyone who wants to save his life will lose it; but anyone who loses his life for my sake, that man will save it. What gain, then, is it for a man to have won the whole world and to have lost or ruined his very self? For if anyone is ashamed of me and of my words, of him the Son of Man will be ashamed when he comes in his own glory and in the glory of the Father and the holy angels."

(Luke 9:23-26)

Deep - ly trou - bled by these words

INWARD JOURNEY

DEEPLY TROUBLED BY THESE WORDS,
DEEPLY TROUBLED BY THESE WORDS.
 Soft words telling of love and freedom,
 Firm words spoken to challenge and correct,
 Questioning words drawing us to search and find.

DEEPLY TROUBLED BY THESE WORDS,
DEEPLY TROUBLED BY THESE WORDS.
 Hillside words of happiness and peace,
 Garden words of life and hope,
 Seashore words of vision and dreams.

DEEPLY TROUBLED BY THESE WORDS,
DEEPLY TROUBLED BY THESE WORDS.
 Desert words of pain and anguish,
 Jordan words of sin and mercy,
 Nazareth words of questing and longing.

DEEPLY TROUBLED BY THESE WORDS,
DEEPLY TROUBLED BY THESE WORDS.
 Cana words of dance and wine,
 Temple words of wisdom and counsel,
 Pilgrim words of whys and wherefores.

DEEPLY TROUBLED BY THESE WORDS,
DEEPLY TROUBLED BY THESE WORDS.
 Enabling words of reverence and affection,
 Spirit words of love and gentleness,
 Personal words of heart and mind.

Deep - ly trou - bled by these words

PRAYER

Jesus, let your words touch our hearts and our lives. We long to truly hear and obey. Be with us; grant us the grace to listen with reverence and anticipation. Guide us by your law of love. Amen.

QUOTATIONS

Cold words freeze people, and hot words scorch them, and bitter words make them bitter, and wrathful words make them wrathful. Kind words also produce their own image on men's souls; and a beautiful image it is. They soothe and quiet, and comfort the hearer. *(Blaise Pascal)*[88]

I soothe my conscience now with the thought that it is better for hard words to be on paper than that Mummy should carry them in her heart. *(Anne Frank)*[89]

There are words which divide and words which unite, words which one can artificially produce and arbitrarily determine, and words which always were—or miraculously are—born anew. Words which unknot the whole to explain the part, and words which implore those who listen to them to go and do that which they proclaim. Words which illuminate a small thing by opening to the light only a part of reality, and words which make us wise by singing out the multiplicity in One.

There are words which "fence off" and isolate. There are also, however, words which make an individual thing transparent so that we can see through to the Infinity of all reality. They are like sea shells in which, no matter how small they themselves are, the ocean of Infinity thunders. They illuminate us, not we them. They have power over us because they are gifts of God—not the makings of men—even if perhaps they do come to us through men.

Some words are clear because they are mysteriously flat and colorless. They are sufficient for our minds. With these we can have power over things. Other words may be obscure because they call forth the blinding brightness of the secret of things. These words climb from our hearts and resound in hymns. They open the door to great deeds and they sit in judgment over eternities. These words that spring from the heart—that have power over us—the words that implore one, the glorifying words that have been given us—I would like to call the *"Urwörte,"* the great words. The rest we can call the fabricated, the technical, the useful words. *(Karl Rahner)*[90]

Silence

MANTRA: **Be still! Know that I am God**

SOURCE: Psalm 46

God is for us a refuge and strength,
a helper close at hand, in time of distress:
so we shall not fear though the earth should rock,
though the mountains fall into the depths of the sea,
even though its waters rage and foam,
even though the mountains be shaken by its waves.

The Lord of hosts is with us:
the God of Jacob is our stronghold.

The waters of a river give joy to God's city,
the holy place where the Most High dwells.
God is within, it cannot be shaken;
God will help it at the dawning of the day.
Nations are in tumult, kingdoms are shaken:
he lifts his voice, the earth shrinks away.

The Lord of hosts is with us:
the God of Jacob is our stronghold.

Come, consider the words of the Lord,
the redoubtable deeds he has done on the earth.
He puts an end to wars over all the earth;
the bow he breaks, the spear he snaps.
He burns the shields with fire.
"Be still and know that I am God,
supreme among the nations, supreme on the earth!"

The Lord of hosts is with us:
the God of Jacob is our stronghold.

PARALLEL REFERENCES

Now he was standing one day by the Lake of Gennesaret, with the crowd pressing around him listening to the word of God, when he caught sight of two boats close to the bank. The fishermen had gone out of them and were washing their nets. He got into one of the boats — it was Simon's — and asked him to put out a little from the shore. Then he sat down and taught the crowds from the boat.

(Luke 5:1-3)

So stay awake, because you do not know when the master of the house is coming, evening, midnight, cockcrow, dawn; if he comes unexpectedly, he must not find you asleep. And what I say to you I say to all: Stay awake! *(Mark 13:35-37)*

Be still! Know that I am God

INWARD JOURNEY

> BE STILL! KNOW THAT I AM GOD,
> BE STILL! KNOW THAT I AM GOD.
>> See the stillness of the stars and learn,
>> Touch the calmness of the lake and trust,
>> Smell the gentle breeze and hope.
>
> BE STILL! KNOW THAT I AM GOD,
> BE STILL! KNOW THAT I AM GOD.
>> Embrace the rose petals — tranquillity,
>> Savor the silence of the brook,
>> Stalk the unsuspecting autumn woods.
>
> BE STILL! KNOW THAT I AM GOD,
> BE STILL! KNOW THAT I AM GOD.
>> Dwell in the solitude of presence,
>> Ground your heart in darkened love,
>> Trod the back roads, hidden caverns.
>
> BE STILL! KNOW THAT I AM GOD,
> BE STILL! KNOW THAT I AM GOD.
>> Listen to cracks and crevices,
>> Prod under rocks treasuring secrets,
>> Whisper your desire and be filled.

Be still! Know that I am God

PRAYER

Lord, may we come to know that you are our God. In the silence of our hearts come to visit and fill us with yourself. Grant us the gift of listening; then draw us to build your kingdom of peace and love. Amen.

QUOTATIONS

Do you suppose that, because we cannot hear Him, He is silent?
(St. Teresa of Avila)[91]

To know silence perfectly is to know music. *(Carl Sandburg)*[92]

Silent music,
In that nocturnal tranquility and silence and in that knowledge of
the divine light the soul becomes aware of Wisdom's wonderful
harmony and sequence in the variety of His creatures and works.
Each of them is endowed with a certain likeness of God and in its
own way gives voice to what God is in it. So creatures will be for the
soul a harmonious symphony of sublime music surpassing all con-
certs and melodies of the world. *(St. John of the Cross)*[93]

Inner silence is for our race a difficult achievement. *(C. S. Lewis)*[94]

Every secret is told, every crime is punished, every virtue rewarded,
every wrong redressed, in silence and certainty.
                                        (Ralph Waldo Emerson)[95]

The whole of space is filled, even though sounds can be heard with
a dense silence which is not an absence of sound but is a positive
object of sensation; it is the secret world, the world of Love who
holds us in his arms from the beginning. *(Simone Weil)*[96]

Renewal

MANTRA: **Renew the face of the earth**

SOURCE: Psalm 104:27-35

All of these [creatures] look to you
to give them their food in due season.
You give it, they gather it up:
you open your hand, they have their fill.

You hide your face, they are dismayed;
you take back your spirit, they die,
returning to the dust from which they came.
You send forth your spirit, they are created;
and you renew the face of the earth.

May the glory of the Lord last for ever!
May the Lord rejoice in his works!
He looks on the earth and it trembles;
the mountains send forth smoke at his touch.

I will sing to the Lord all my life,
make music to my God while I live.
May my thoughts be pleasing to him.
I find my joy in the Lord.
Let sinners vanish from the earth
and the wicked exist no more.

Bless the Lord, my soul!

PARALLEL REFERENCES

So Jesus spoke to them again:
  "I have come
  so that they may have life
  and have it to the full." *(John 10:7, 10)*

A feeling of expectancy had grown among the people, who were beginning to think that John might be the Christ, so John declared before them all, "I baptize you with water, but someone is coming, someone who is more powerful than I am, and I am not fit to undo the strap of his sandals; he will baptize you with the Holy Spirit and fire. His winnowing fan is in his hand to clear his threshing floor and to gather the wheat into his barn; but the chaff he will burn in a fire that will never go out." As well as this, there were many other things he said to exhort the people and to announce the Good News to them. *(Luke 3:15-18)*

Re - new the face of the earth

INWARD JOURNEY

RENEW THE FACE OF THE EARTH,
RENEW THE FACE OF THE EARTH.
Though scarred and battered, come,
Though broken and destitute, come,
Though discourteous and bitter, come.

RENEW THE FACE OF THE EARTH,
RENEW THE FACE OF THE EARTH.
Despite hostility and war, come,
Despite terror and violence, come,
Despite insult and cruelty, come.

RENEW THE FACE OF THE EARTH,
RENEW THE FACE OF THE EARTH.
And people will dance and sing once again,
And lakes and lands will rejoice and be glad,
And city and country will become our home.

RENEW THE FACE OF THE EARTH,
RENEW THE FACE OF THE EARTH.
For the sake of those who love you,
For the sake of those who fear you,
For the sake of those who hope in you.

Re - new the face of the earth

PRAYER

Lord, send your Spirit into our lives and our world; then we shall
live. Remember your promise of long ago — do not forget your people. We have marred our hearts and your garden; heal and restore
us to your image and likeness. Have mercy, Lord.

The criticism and attack on institutions, which we have witnessed, has made one thing plain, that society gains nothing whilst a man, not himself renovated, attempts to renovate things around him: he has become tediously good in some particular but negligent or narrow in the rest; and hypocrisy and vanity are often the disgusting result. *(Ralph Waldo Emerson)*[97]

He who lives and moves in Christ takes the only road there is out of the labyrinthian tangle of the world into the freedom and new creation in God. *(Romano Guardini)*[98]

When a person continues to live with others, simultaneously also with Christ, his relations to the others will change, if only in that he becomes increasingly patient, more understanding, kinder, but also more alert, less gullible, and better able to judge character and worth, whatever his natural limitations happen to be. All this is true, but still not the essential difference. The person himself is changed by his daily contact with Christ, becoming more and more similar to his model. The believer remains in his profession; he remains the same trader, postman, doctor that he was, with the same duties. The machine does not function better in his hand than in that of another; the diagnosis is not easier than it was, yet work performed in Christ is somehow different. No longer overestimated, but properly evaluated, it assumes a new dignity and earnestness; is performed with a new conscientiousness. The same holds true for worries and pain and other human need. The difference is indefinable, visible only in the result: here an illness or loss borne with quiet heroism, there an old enmity healed. In Christ all things are changed. *(Romano Guardini)*[99]

A man who has been in another world does not come back unchanged. *(C. S. Lewis)*[100]

Indwelling

MANTRA: **And the Father is in me**

SOURCE: John 14:9-17

"To have seen me is to have seen the Father,
so how can you say, 'Let us see the Father'?
Do you not believe
that I am in the Father and the Father is in me?
The words I say to you I do not speak as from myself:
it is the Father, living in me, who is doing this work.
You must believe me when I say
that I am in the Father and the Father is in me;
believe it on the evidence of this work, if for no other reason.
I tell you most solemnly,
whoever believes in me
will perform the same works as I do myself,
he will perform even greater works,
because I am going to the Father.
Whatever you ask for in my name I will do,
so that the Father may be glorified in the Son.
If you ask for anything in my name,
I will do it.
If you love me you will keep my commandments.
I shall ask the Father,
and he will give you another Advocate
to be with you for ever,
that Spirit of truth
whom the world can never receive
since it neither sees nor knows him;
but you know him,
because he is with you, he is in you."

PARALLEL REFERENCES

As soon as Jesus was baptized he came up from the water, and suddenly the heavens opened and he saw the Spirit of God descending like a dove and coming down on him. And a voice spoke from heaven, "This is my Son, the Beloved; my favor rests on him."

(Matthew 3:16-17)

When the sixth hour came there was darkness over the whole land until the ninth hour. And at the ninth hour Jesus cried out in a loud voice, "Eloi, Eloi, lama sabachthani?" which means, "My God, my God, why have you deserted me?" *(Mark 15:33-34)*

And the Fa - ther is in me

INWARD JOURNEY

AND THE FATHER IS IN ME,
AND THE FATHER IS IN ME.
On dusty roads in distant lands,
On stormy seas with faithless men,
On quiet eves far from home.

AND THE FATHER IS IN ME,
AND THE FATHER IS IN ME.
Desirous to share my every deed,
Touching the sick through my embrace,
Consoling the broken with loving gaze.

AND THE FATHER IS IN ME,
AND THE FATHER IS IN ME.
Showing the way moment by moment,
Stirring my heart to taste daily pain,
Directing my way to justice and peace.

AND THE FATHER IS IN ME,
AND THE FATHER IS IN ME.

In the darkness of faith seeming absent,
In the gentleness of hope with so many "not yets,"
In the graciousness of love with so few returns.

PRAYER

My Father, you dwell within me and in all creation. What mystery here, incomprehensible to our finite minds. Grace us to live in your presence; heal our blindness and deafness. As you live in us, may we live in you and from this mutuality establish your Kingdom through service and love. Father, present within me, hear this prayer. Amen.

QUOTATIONS

The place which Jesus takes in our soul he will nevermore vacate, for in us is his home of homes, and it is the greatest delight for him to dwell there. This was a delectable and restful sight, for it is so in truth forevermore; and to contemplate this while we are here is most pleasing to God, and very great profit to us. And the soul who thus contemplates is made like to him who is contemplated, and united to him in rest and peace. And it was a singular joy and bliss to me that I saw him sit, for the contemplation of this sitting revealed to me the certainty that he will dwell in us forever; and I knew truly that it was he who had revealed everything to me before. And when I had contemplated this with great attention, our Lord very humbly revealed words to me, without voice and without opening of lips, as he had done before and said very seriously: Know it well, it was no hallucination which you saw today, but accept and believe it and hold firmly to it, and you will not be overcome. *(Julian of Norwich)*[101]

What characterizes Jesus is the way his whole life is concentrated in this confidence that the Father is near to him. Because God is not hidden at a remote distance, this familiarity and exclusivity is both possible and legitimate. Moreover, it heightens and brings out the whole drama of the cross, where Jesus is abandoned by the Father in whom he has placed all his trust. *(Jon Sobrino)*[102]

Alongside this movement of Jesus toward the Father in total trust and confidence is Jesus' awareness of the Father's movement toward him. The Father has given him a mission, and Jesus' response is one of total *obedience.* His awareness of a mission from the Father is so patent that the Synoptic Gospels do not talk about it explicitly even though it pervades every page. Jesus' life makes sense only in terms of his awareness of this mission. Later on, Paul's theology will describe Jesus as the *one sent* by the Father and the Johannine writings will say the same thing. *(Jon Sobrino)*[103]

NOTES

1. *The Poems of Gerard Manley Hopkins,* 4th ed., ed. W. H. Gardner and N. H. MacKenzie (Oxford: Oxford University Press, 1967) 27.

2. "Flower in the Crannied Wall," in George K. Anderan and William E. Buckler (eds.), *The Literature of England: An Anthology and a History* (Glenview, Ill.: Scott, Foresman and Company, 1953) 901.

3. "The Blade of Grass," in Joseph Katz (ed.), *The Complete Poems of Stephen Crane* (Ithaca, N.Y.: Cornell University Press, 1972) 20.

4. G. K. Chesterton, *St. Francis of Assisi* (New York: Doubleday Image Book, 1957) 78.

5. Dee Brown, *Bury My Heart at Wounded Knee* (New York: Holt, Rinehart & Winston, 1970) 77.

6. Dante Alighieri, *The Divine Comedy,* trans. Lawrence Grant White (New York: Pantheon Books, 1948) 181.

7. "Death," in Anderan and Buckler, *The Literature of England,* 328.

8. Hermann Hesse, *Siddhartha,* trans. Hilda Rosner (New York: New Directions Publishing Corp., 1951) 104.

9. Ladislaus Boros, *Hidden God,* trans. Erika Young (New York: The Seabury Press, Inc., 1971) 40.

10. Antoine de Saint-Exupéry, *The Little Prince* (New York: Harcourt, Brace & World, 1943) 70.

11. Soren Kierkegaard, *Philosophical Fragments,* trans. David Swenson (Princeton: Princeton University Press, 1962) 64.

12. Gerald Vann, *St. Thomas Aquinas* (New York: Benziger Bros., 1947) 24.

13. *The Collected Works of St. John of the Cross,* trans. Kieran Kavanaugh and Otilio Rodriguez (Washington: ICS Publications, 1973) 244–45.

14. *Meister Eckhart,* trans. Raymond B. Blakney (New York: Harper Torchbooks, 1941) 89.

15. *The Complete Works of St. Teresa of Jesus,* trans. E. Allison Peers (London: Sheed & Ward Ltd., 1944) 1:290–91.

16. *Ibid.,* 2:173.

17. Paul Horgan, *A Distant Trumpet* (New York: Farrar, Straus & Cudahy, 1951) 241.

18. William McNamara, *The Human Adventure* (New York: Doubleday and Company, 1974) 188.

19. "Self-Reliance," in *The Selected Writings of Ralph Waldo Emerson,* ed. Brooks Atkinson (New York: The Modern Library, 1940) 158.

20. Romano Guardini, *The Lord* (Chicago: Henry Regnery Company, 1954) 34.

21. "The Tiger," in Anderan and Buckler, *The Literature of England,* 676.

22. *The Divine Comedy,* 140.

23. Joseph Conrad, *The Nigger of the Narcissus* (New York: Dell Publishing Company, Inc., 1960) xvi.

24. *Final Harvest: Emily Dickinson's Poems,* ed. Thomas H. Johnson (Boston: Little, Brown and Company, 1961) 48.

25. *The Divine Comedy,* 160.

26. *The Poems of Gerard Manley Hopkins,* 28.

27. Jean Montaurier, *A Passage Through Fire* (New York: Holt, Rinehart & Winston, 1965) 341.

28. *The Divine Comedy,* 184.

29. *The Confessions of St. Augustine,* trans. John K. Ryan (New York: Doubleday Image Book, 1960) 363.

30. *The Complete Works of St. Teresa of Jesus,* 1:313.

31. "Beauty," in *The Selected Writings of Ralph Waldo Emerson,* 463.

32. Fynn, *Mister God, This Is Anna* (New York: Rinehart and Winston, 1974) 158.

33. "Trinity Sunday," in *The Poetical Works of Herbert and Vaughan* (Boston: Houghton, Mifflin & Co., 1864) 74.

34. C. S. Lewis, *That Hideous Strength* (New York: The Macmillan Company, 1946) 148.

35. Félix Martí-Ibáñez, *The Crystal Arrow* (New York: Clarkson N. Potter, Inc., 1964) 14.

36. *The Divine Comedy,* 149.

37. "Ulysses," in Anderan and Buckler, *The Literature of England,* 847.

38. "Friendship," in *The Selected Writings of Ralph Waldo Emerson,* 230.

39. *Confessions,* 220.

40. "Manners," in *The Selected Writings of Ralph Waldo Emerson,* 399.

41. Bernard Lonergan, "The Dimensions of Meaning," *Collection: Papers by Bernard Lonergan,* ed. F. E. Crowe (New York: Herder and Herder, 1967) 264.

42. Walter Kerr, *The Decline of Pleasure* (New York: Simon & Schuster, Inc., 1962) 291.

43. *The Cloud of Unknowing and the Book of Privy Counseling,* ed. William Johnston (New York: Doubleday Image Book, 1973) 64.

44. *King Lear,* Act I, sc. 1, ll. 56–62.

45. Robert Bolt, *A Man for All Seasons* (New York: Vintage Books, 1960) 81.

46. *Beowulf,* ll. 2292–93, in *An Anthology of Old English Poetry,* trans. Charles W. Kennedy (New York: Oxford University Press, 1960).

47. *The Divine Comedy,* 160.

48. Romano Guardini, *The Living God,* trans. Stanley Godman (New York: Panthcon Books, Inc., 1957) 33–34.

49. *The Simone Weil Reader,* ed. George A. Panichas (New York: David McKay Company, Inc., 1977) 51.

50. *The Divine Comedy,* 188.

51. "Love," in *The Poetical Works of Herbert and Vaughan,* 230.

52. Murray Bodo, *Francis: The Journey and the Dream* (Cincinnati: St. Anthony Messenger Press, 1972) 18.

53. John Henry Newman, *Certain Difficulties Felt by Anglicans in Catholic Teaching* (New York: Longmans, 1908).

54. *Simone Weil Reader,* 51.

55. "The Pulley," in *The Poetical Works of Herbert and Vaughan,* 192.

56. Thomas Merton, *The Seven Storey Mountain* (New York: Harcourt, Brace and Company, 1948) 203.

57. *The Hound of Heaven* (New York: Dodd, Mead and Co., 1967) 59–60.

58. *Confessions,* 63.

59. C. S. Lewis, *A Grief Observed* (New York: The Seabury Press, Inc., 1961) 54.

60. C. S. Lewis, *The Last Battle* (New York: The Macmillan Company, 1954) 98.

61. Newman to Mrs. Bowden. Cited in Meriol Trevor, *Newman: The Pillar of the Cloud* (New York: Doubleday and Company, 1962) 359.

62. Whittaker Chambers, *Witness* (New York: Random House, 1952) 532.

63. Alessandro Manzoni, *The Betrothed,* trans. Daniel J. Connor (New York: The Macmillan Company, 1926) 7.

64. "Rabbi ben Ezra," in Anderan and Buckler, *The Literature of England,* 929.

65. Quoted in Thomas A. Kane, *The Healing Touch of Affirmation* (Whitinsville, Mass.: Affirmation Books, 1976) 17.

66. *The Lord,* 232.

67. Romano Guardini, *The Life of Faith,* trans. John Chapin (Westminster, Md.: The Newman Press, 1961) 106.

68. "Self-Reliance," in *The Selected Writings of Ralph Waldo Emerson,* 157.

69. Raïssa Maritain, *We Have Been Friends Together* (New York: Green and Co., 1942) 172.

70. Henri J. Nouwen, *The Genesee Diary: Report from a Trappist Monastery* (New York: Doubleday and Company, 1976) 59.

71. Fynn, *Mister God,* 172.

72. *We Have Been Friends Together,* 100.

73. C. S. Lewis, *Mere Christianity* (New York: The Macmillan Company, 1947) 38.

74. *The Complete Works of St. Teresa of Jesus,* 1:37.

75. *Julian of Norwich: Showings,* trans. Edmond Colledge, O.S.A.,

and James Walsh, S.J., Classics of Western Spirituality (New York: Paulist Press, 1978) 237–38.

76. *Confessions,* 260.

77. Jon Sobrino, *Christology at the Crossroads,* trans. John Drury (Maryknoll, N.Y.: Orbis Books, 1978) 112.

78. *Confessions,* 43.

79. "Pied Beauty," in *Poems and Prose of Gerard Manley Hopkins,* selected by W. H. Gardner (London: Penguin Books, 1958) 30.

80. Ruth Mary Fox, "Some Did Return," *Some Did Return* (Fort Lauderdale, Fla.: Wake-Brooke House, 1976) 93.

81. Georges Bernanos, *The Diary of a Country Priest,* trans. Pamela Morris (New York: Doubleday and Company, 1954) 140.

82. Simone Weil, *Waiting for God,* trans. Emma Craufurd (New York: Harper Colophon Books, 1951) 94.

83. Quoted in Roger Lancelyn Green and Walter Hooper, *C. S. Lewis: A Biography* (New York: Harcourt Brace Jovanovich, 1974) 106.

84. *Christology at the Crossroads,* 262.

85. C. S. Lewis, *Surprised by Joy* (New York: Harcourt, Brace & World, 1955) 229.

86. *Confessions,* 63.

87. *The Collected Works of St. John of the Cross,* 487.

88. Quoted in *Bits and Pieces,* August 1976 (Fairfield, N.J.: The Economics Press).

89. *Anne Frank: The Diary of a Young Girl,* trans. B. M. Mooyart (New York: Doubleday and Company, 1952) 141.

90. Karl Rahner, "Priest and Poet," *The Word: Readings in Theology* (New York: P. J. Kenedy and Sons, 1964) 4–5.

91. *The Complete Works of St. Teresa of Jesus,* 2:103.

92. "To Know Silence Perfectly," in *Complete Poems of Carl Sandburg* (New York: Harcourt, Brace and World, Inc., 1950) 410.

93. *The Collected Works of St. John of the Cross,* 472.

94. C. S. Lewis, *Perelandra* (New York: The Macmillan Company, 1944) 140.

95. "Compensation," in *The Selected Writings of Ralph Waldo Emerson,* 175.

96. *Simone Weil Reader,* 87.

97. "New England Reformers," in *The Selected Writings of Ralph Waldo Emerson,* 455.

98. Source unknown.

99. *The Lord,* 446.

100. *Perelandra,* 10.

101. *Julian of Norwich: Showings,* 164.

102. *Christology at the Crossroads,* 72.

103. *Ibid.*

A trilogy on prayer by Bishop Robert F. Morneau—

OUR FATHER REVISITED

Dividing the *Our Father* into eight sections, Bishop Morneau offers four reflections on each part, providing rich material for four hours of prayers during eight days. The book is introduced by practical notes on the principles of prayer.

This is an ideal text for a private, directed, or traditional retreat.

One reviewer states: "For the price you will not find a better book to use for personal meditation."

78 pages, paperback, $2.95

TRINITY SUNDAY REVISITED
Patterns for Prayer

Here Bishop Morneau provides thirty-two themes for prayer drawn from the poem "Trinity Sunday" by George Herbert, a seventeenth-century Anglican clergyman and poet. This volume offers more than enough inspirational material for a retreat, a day of quiet, or an hour of meditation. Ten practical principles of prayer form the Introduction.

A reviewer comments: "It is a pleasure to recommend so valuable a treatise on prayer and spirituality. The publisher has kept the price so moderate that many libraries will be able to afford multiple copies. Clergy and laity can profit from this book."

96 pages, paperback, $2.95

DISCOVERING GOD'S PRESENCE

Comprising this volume are fifteen of Bishop Morneau's articles that appeared in *Contemplative Review, Review for Religious, Sisters Today,* and *Spiritual Life.* The single reflection unifying these essays is that the more lovingly conscious we are of God's presence, the more meaningful and joyful our lives will be. This fundamental transforming truth the author helps us to discover in poetry and prayer, in struggle and success, in living and dying, and in a multitude of divine surprises.

187 pages, paperback, $5.95

THE LITURGICAL PRESS
Collegeville, Minnesota 56321